Cite-Checker

Second Edition

ASPEN PUBLISHERS

Cite-Checker
A Hands-On Guide to Learning Citation Form

Second Edition

Deborah E. Bouchoux, Esq.
Georgetown University

 Wolters Kluwer
Law & Business

AUSTIN   BOSTON   CHICAGO   NEW YORK   THE NETHERLANDS

Aspen Publishers
Attn: Permissions Department
76 Ninth Avenue, 7th Floor
New York, NY 10011-5201

To contact Customer Care, e-mail customer.care@aspenpublishers.com,
call 1-800-234-1660, fax 1-800-901-9075, or mail correspondence to:

Aspen Publishers
Attn: Order Department
PO Box 990
Frederick, MD 21705

Printed in the United States of America.

1 2 3 4 5 6 7 8 9 0

ISBN 978-0-7355-7122-8

Library of Congress Cataloging-in-Publication Data

Bouchoux, Deborah E., 1950-
Cite-Checker : a hands-on guide to learning citation form/Deborah E.
Bouchoux. — 2nd ed.
     p. cm.
   Includes index.
   ISBN 978-0-7355-7122-8
   1. Citation of legal authorities — United States. I. Title.
KF245.B68 2008
340.01'48 — dc22

                                                                        2007040250

About Wolters Kluwer Law & Business

Wolters Kluwer Law & Business is a leading provider of research information and workflow solutions in key specialty areas. The strength of the individual brands of Aspen Publishers, CCH, Kluwer Law International and Loislaw are aligned within Wolters Kluwer Law & Business to provide comprehensive, in-depth solutions and expert-authored content for the legal, professional and education markets.

CCH was founded in 1913 and has served more than four generations of business professionals and their clients. The CCH products in the Wolters Kluwer Law & Business group are highly regarded electronic and print resources for legal, securities, antitrust and trade regulation, government contracting, banking, pension, payroll, employment and labor, and health-care reimbursement and compliance professionals.

Aspen Publishers is a leading information provider for attorneys, business professionals and law students. Written by preeminent authorities, Aspen products offer analytical and practical information in a range of specialty practice areas from securities law and intellectual property to mergers and acquisitions and pension/benefits. Aspen's trusted legal education resources provide professors and students with high-quality, up-to-date and effective resources for successful instruction and study in all areas of the law.

Kluwer Law International supplies the global business community with comprehensive English-language international legal information. Legal practitioners, corporate counsel and business executives around the world rely on the Kluwer Law International journals, loose-leafs, books and electronic products for authoritative information in many areas of international legal practice.

Loislaw is a premier provider of digitized legal content to small law firm practitioners of various specializations. Loislaw provides attorneys with the ability to quickly and efficiently find the necessary legal information they need, when and where they need it, by facilitating access to primary law as well as state-specific law, records, forms and treatises.

Wolters Kluwer Law & Business, a unit of Wolters Kluwer, is headquartered in New York and Riverwoods, Illinois. Wolters Kluwer is a leading multinational publisher and information services company.

Dedication

For my husband, Donald, and our children
Meaghan, Elizabeth, Patrick, and Robert

Contents

Introduction

The task of checking one's own citations or those of another author to ensure they comply with the format of *The Bluebook: A Uniform System of Citation* (Columbia Law Review Ass'n et al. eds., 18th ed. 2005) is usually called cite-checking or "Bluebooking." *The Bluebook* consists of nearly 400 pages of rules. Some of these rules are poorly explained while others are inconsistent and arbitrary. For example, when sending a reader to a page within an immediately preceding authority, one uses the form "*id.* at 16." However, when sending the reader to a paragraph or section within an immediately preceding authority, one uses "*id.* § 16" or "*id.* ¶ 16." In other words, one cannot use the word "at" before a section symbol or paragraph sign. Why? No one knows. Similarly, one must place a comma after the title of a law review article or annotation but not after a book title. These and myriad other inconsistencies make cite-checking a frustrating task for nearly all legal writers.

For practitioners, the task is complicated even further by the fact that *The Bluebook* is designed for use by law students or those writing law review or law journal articles. Most of the examples given in *The Bluebook* are presented in a particular style of typeface, called "large and small capitals," that practitioners do not use. Moreover, full case names throughout nearly all of *The Bluebook* are neither underscored nor italicized, while practitioners always underscore or italicize case names.

In sum, practitioners have lacked a clear and brief guide to citation form designed exclusively for them. After years of teaching legal research and providing numerous in-house seminars for practitioners at law firms, government agencies, and in-house legal departments, it became clear to me that practitioners were woefully underserved by *The Bluebook*. It is the author's hope that this book fills the need for a short and simple guide to the most common types of citations used by practitioners so that the task of cite-checking will be easier and less frustrating.

Use of This Book

All legal authorities can be categorized into one of two broad categories: primary authorities and secondary authorities. Primary authorities include cases, statutes, constitutions, and administrative regulations (such as regulations of the FDA or FCC). Nearly everything else (including books, articles, and law dictionaries) is a secondary authority. Legal writers typically prefer to cite primary authorities rather than secondary authorities because courts are bound to follow primary authorities from their jurisdiction, assuming these authorities are relevant or "on point." Primary authorities are thus usually referred to as "binding" or "mandatory," while secondary authorities are described as "persuasive."

This book is arranged in a building-block approach. First, users should master primary authorities, namely, the most frequently cited authorities: cases and statutes. They will then be ready to move on to secondary authorities and then to the use of quotations, signals, and short forms. In each instance, *The Bluebook* rules are explained, and then examples (most of which are fictitious) are given.

For the most thorough mastery of citation form, users should start at Chapter 1 and continue reading through the text, doing the pertinent exercises along the way. An answer key for each exercise is printed at the back of this book. While users will quickly be able to memorize some citation forms, most legal writers continually refer to *The Bluebook* to ensure a citation is correct. No one expects legal writers to have mastered all of *The Bluebook* rules together with their numerous exceptions. Thus, continual reference to *The Bluebook* while preparing answers to the exercises herein and while on the job is expected.

As new topics are introduced throughout this book, references are given to the guiding rules or sections in *The Bluebook*. Thus, a reference to "Rule 15" refers to Rule 15 in *The Bluebook*, while a reference to "B9" refers to Bluepages Rule 9 of *The Bluebook*. References to tables, such as Table T.1, refer to tables in *The Bluebook*.

When dates in sample citations are shown as "(19xx)," acceptable formats include dates from other centuries if appropriate.

Scope of This Book

This guide covers most of the basic citation rules, giving several examples. It is impossible, however, to give complete coverage to *Bluebook* rules without nearly duplicating the size of the original *Bluebook*. Moreover, there are authorities that even *The Bluebook* does not address. When confronted with such material, *The Bluebook* suggests that one try to locate an analogous authority, always being guided by the principle that a writer must ensure a reader can find the cited authority quickly and reliably.

Although putting citations into their proper form is the hardest component of cite-checking, there is one other component to the task: "Shepardizing" (if using the LexisNexis computer research system) or "KeyCiting" (if using the Westlaw computer research system), which are methods to ensure authorities cited are still good law. This book does not cover Shepardizing or KeyCiting. It is designed solely for the purpose of assisting legal writers in proper citation form. For information on Shepardizing or KeyCiting (which are now done electronically rather than manually in nearly every law firm and legal department), consult textbooks on legal research or access Lexis Nexis's website at http://web.lexis.com/lawschoolreg/tutorials/shepards and use the tutorial to learn how to Shepardize. Alternatively, access Westlaw's site at http://west.thomson.com/keycite/guides for West's User Guide to KeyCiting and other product information. Finally, most of the examples in this book are fictitious.

Please note the Internet resources are of a time sensitive nature and URL addresses may often change or be deleted.

Acknowledgments

No publication is the product solely of its author. Many individuals contributed significantly to the development of this guide to citation form. As always, my first thoughts and gratitude go to Susan M. Sullivan, Program Director of the Paralegal Program at the University of San Diego, who provided me with my first teaching opportunity. Sue is a valued colleague and a dear friend.

My former program director, Gloria Silvers of the Paralegal Studies Program at Georgetown University in Washington, DC, has been of invaluable assistance and encouragement to me.

Special thanks to my many students who, with their probing questions and curiosity, prompted me to continue trying to master the intricacies of *The Bluebook*. The reviewers who evaluated the original manuscript of this publication provided prompt and clear analysis and must, therefore, be recognized:

Ms. Suzanne Bailey, Western Illinois University
Mr. Adam Epstein, University of Tennessee
Mr. John Frank, Chippewa Valley Technical College
Mr. Chris Whaley, Roane State Community College
Ms. Donna Bookin, Mercy College
Ms. Julia O. Tryk, Cuyahoga Community College
Ms. Patricia Adongo, University of LaVerne
Ms. Barbara Ricker, Andover College

I would like to express my most sincere appreciation to the following individuals at Aspen Publishers who provided continued encouragement and support throughout the development of *Cite-Checker*: David Herzig, Acquisitions Editor; Betsy Kenny, Development Editor; Kaesmene Harrison Banks, Editor; Lauren Arnest, copy editor; and Jan Cocker, proofreader.

Finally, deepest thanks and love to my husband Don and our children Meaghan, Elizabeth, Patrick, and Robert, for their unflagging patience and understanding while I continually pored over *The Bluebook* while writing this guide to citation form.

I would also like to thank Thomson/West for its permission to reprint Figure 3-4, the map of the thirteen federal judicial circuits that appears in Chapter 3.

1

Introduction to Cite-Checking

The Task of Cite-Checking

A 300-plus page book entitled *The Bluebook: A Uniform System of Citation* (Columbia Law Review Ass'n et al. eds., 18th ed. 2005) (*The Bluebook*) is the standard reference tool in the United States for citing legal authorities. Although some states, including California and Michigan, have their own citation systems and many courts have established rules governing citation for documents submitted to them, *The Bluebook* remains the gold standard for citation form throughout the United States.

The principle underlying *The Bluebook* is that citation form for cases, statutes, and other authorities should be consistent throughout the entire United States, so that a practitioner in Ohio can submit a brief to a New York court, and all readers will know how and where to locate the authorities referred to in the document. The task of placing citations in their proper format is typically called "cite-checking" or "Bluebooking."

Why must a practitioner learn the intricate and difficult rules of citation form? First, citation form communicates critical information to a reader because it allows a reader to locate and review authorities referred to in a legal document. Thus, an organized, systematic, uniform system of citation is needed so all law practitioners cite cases, statutes, and other authorities the same way each time they are used. Second, while incorrect citation form is not an act of legal malpractice, it reflects badly on you and your firm or company, much the same way a spelling error has a disproportionately negative effect on a reader. Carelessness in citation form may lead a reader to believe you are equally careless in your analysis of the law. Law firms and departments strive for excellence and professionalism to best serve their clients. Correct citation form is an integral part of this goal. Nevertheless, there is tremendous inconsistency in citation form often contributed to by courts themselves, which frequently use incorrect citation form in their own published opinions. Similarly, law book publishers contribute to misunderstanding of citation form by often using incorrect citation form, typically in an effort to save space and reduce printing costs.

Practice Tip

✓ Do not rely on citation form used in published case reports or other legal authorities, including Lexis and Westlaw. To save space or to emphasize market brand, these forms are often incorrect. Use *The Bluebook.*

▓ *The Bluebook*

Introduction

The Bluebook is the accepted "bible" for citation form (unless court rules dictate otherwise). Yet its myriad rules are awkwardly phrased, haphazardly arranged, and seemingly contradictory Why? *The Bluebook* was originally intended as a short guide to aid law students in preparing citations in their scholarly writings. Eventually, as legal authorities proliferated, so did the rules in *The Bluebook*. Additionally, it began to be accepted as the citation form authority for practitioners as well as for those engaged in scholarly writing, although the presentation style used for scholarly writing (a style that used LARGE AND SMALL CAPITALS) could not be reproduced by practitioners who were typing their documents rather than having them professionally typeset. Thus, one citation guide attempts to fit vastly differing needs.

Moreover, *The Bluebook*'s coverage may simply be too broad. In providing information about citing to Swiss civil law cases, the East African Court of

Appeal, and Tasmanian Statutes, little space is available to provide examples of far less esoteric citation forms, such as those for New York cases.

Thus, *The Bluebook*'s numerous rules and their exceptions, dual approach, and broad coverage have contributed to frustration for cite-checkers. Moreover, the task of cite-checking is often done at the eleventh hour, making it difficult and pressure-filled. Finally, it requires attention to detail and a high level of concentration to locate minute errors in spacing and abbreviations. All of these factors contribute to an often difficult task. By learning the most frequently used citation rules, however, in a step-by-step approach, you will achieve mastery of this task.

While there are other citation guides, such as *The Maroonbook* (published by the University of Chicago and used primarily in the Chicago metropolitan area), or *ALWD*, a user-friendly citation manual published by the Association of Legal Writing Directors and Professor Darby Dickerson, *The Bluebook* is the most widely adopted system of citation and should be followed unless court rules or law firm or company policy require otherwise.

History of *The Bluebook*

The Bluebook is compiled by the editors of the *Columbia Law Review, Harvard Law Review, University of Pennsylvania Law Review,* and *The Yale Law Journal.* Originally compiled in the mid-1920s, *The Bluebook* was a small pamphlet designed to instruct scholarly writers and the printers of scholarly articles in citation form. Over the years, *The Bluebook* was revised a number of times. The present edition in use is the Eighteenth Edition. Earlier editions have little, if any, practical value and can be discarded. New editions are not released at regularly scheduled intervals but rather when the editors believe changes are needed. The Eighteenth Edition was issued in mid-2005 and includes a number of new features, including changes dictated by new technologies (such as instructions on citing to blogs, the Internet, e-mail correspondence, and DVDs).

Changes in *The Bluebook* over time may result in some citations being incorrect now that may have been correct several years ago when they were first prepared. Thus, exercise care when importing citations from a previously written document into your document. Ensure citations you use conform to present-day *Bluebook* rules.

Organization of *The Bluebook*

Spend a few minutes becoming familiar with the organization of *The Bluebook*. In particular, note the following:

- Examine the Preface to the Eighteenth Edition (pages v and vi). These pages outline changes made in the Eighteenth Edition of *The Bluebook*. When the next edition of *The Bluebook* is issued, examine this section to learn new rules and changes.
- Review the section on light blue paper beginning on page 3, called "the Bluepages." The examples found on pages 3-24 are ready for use by practitioners, meaning there is no need to convert typeface or make other changes to adapt *Bluebook* forms, originally intended for scholarly writers, for use in the "real world." The Bluepages show how to adapt the examples found in the body of *The Bluebook* to the format needed for court documents and legal memoranda. The Bluepages are far more complete and extensive than the prior Practitioners' Notes (found in the Seventeenth Edition) and provide numerous helpful examples.
- Note Table T.1. After setting forth rules about federal court cases, there is a section devoted to citation form for the states, each of which is listed in alphabetical order. A reference is provided for each state's judicial website. Although you will not be given examples, you will be provided with a blueprint for setting up citations for the cases and statutes in each state.
- Table T.10 provides abbreviations for each state. Note that the abbreviations may not conform to your expectation as to how to abbreviate a particular state's name. Similarly, Table T.12 provides abbreviations for the months of the year. These are but two examples of *The Bluebook*'s insistence on uniformity.
- The Index, printed on white paper at the end of *The Bluebook* provides a ready reference to locating information. It is well-organized and complete.
- The outside back cover provides a mini-Index to *The Bluebook*, making it easy to find various rules.

■ New Features of the Eighteenth Edition of *The Bluebook*

The new Eighteenth Edition of *The Bluebook* provides a number of new features, including the following:

- Many user-friendly elements are provided, including the use of the color blue to demonstrate certain examples, the use of spacing guides to show spacing in certain citation formats such as ellipses, "Tips" in the Bluepages, and a mini table of contents at the beginning of each *Bluebook* rule.
- The Bluepages include two useful tables, BT.1, which shows abbreviations to be used for court documents (such as "Aff." for Affidavit) and BT.2, which references some helpful local citation rules and some jurisdiction-specific citation manuals that provide guidance on local citation practices.
- Table T.2, relating to international sources, has nearly doubled in size.
- Many practical and useful citation forms are now given, including citation forms for patents, for various SEC materials (such as annual reports and proxy statements), and for Generally Accepted Accounting Principles (GAAP), forms that practitioners often need.

Practice Tip

✓ Make *The Bluebook* work for you. Use sticky flags to tab the sections you rely on most frequently, such as the Bluepages, Rule 10 (relating to cases), Rule 12 (relating to statutes), Table T.l (providing rules for citing cases and statutes in all U.S. jurisdictions), Table T.6 (providing abbreviations), and the Index (allowing you easy access to the rules you need).

■ Top Ten Tips for Effective Cite-Checking

Because cite-checking is typically an eleventh-hour assignment and requires painstaking attention to detail, the task requires patience and a highly organized approach. The following tips will make your task more manageable.

1. **Highlight all citations.** Your first step should be to take a colored marker and highlight all citations (both primary and secondary authorities) in a document. You may be surprised to discover that after an hour or so, the citations tend to blend into the text of the document, particularly when italics are used rather than underscoring. Thus, if you highlight each citation when you are fresh, you will readily be able to locate and check each citation when your attention may be flagging. Consider using a pink highlighter to mark all cases, blue for statutes, and so forth. A color-coded system will allow you to check all authorities of the same type at once, which may be easier than switching back and forth between different types of authorities.

2. **Get instructions.** If cite-checking for another, ask the author or the supervisor who assigned the cite-checking assignment whether you can assume numbers and dates are correct and that you, therefore, need only check spacing, punctuation, and other format considerations or whether you should do a "top to bottom" check and verify the accuracy of every number and date. When in doubt, err on the side of caution, and do the most thorough check possible. Similarly, ask if the author or the judge to whom the document is being sent has a preference for underscoring rather than italicizing case names and book titles. This will save time later if your first draft uses italics, and the author or judge insists all case names and book titles be underscored.

3. **Ask for help.** If cite-checking for another writer, call or e-mail your colleagues and ask if anyone has done a cite-checking assignment for the particular author and whether the author has any particular preferences or quirks. Similarly, if the document is addressed to a court, ask if anyone has recently filed a document with that court. Using a model will give you a certain comfort level. Save your cite-checked briefs, and make your own model form files.

4. **Know the rules.** Many courts have mandated their own rules for citation form. For example, California Rule of Court 3.1113 provides that court memoranda must conform to the *California Style Manual* or *The Bluebook*. If your document is addressed to a court, determine if such rules exist. If they do, they supersede

The Bluebook rules. To determine whether court rules exist, ask your law librarian (if your firm has one) to call the clerk of the court and inquire, or check the Internet. For home pages of all federal courts, access http://www.uscourts.gov, and follow the instructions to locate rules of court. For state court rules, access http://www.megalaw.com and select "State Law." You may then select the desired state and link directly to its rules of court. Remember to review Table BT.2 in *The Bluebook*, which provides references to local rules that relate to citation form. Also, check Table T.1 of *The Bluebook*, which identifies judicial websites for each state. Similarly, some law firms and law departments have their own practices and procedures for citation form. Ask if such policies exist.

5. **Support your corrections.** As you correct citations in the document, write legibly so the individual who later word processes the document can readily make the appropriate corrections. Note on your draft the page of *The Bluebook* or the pertinent rule that supports your correction. For example, if the author has used a broken line for the subsequent history signal rev'd en banc and your review of page 10 of *The Bluebook* shows it as rev'd en banc, jot "page 10" near your correction. If the author later challenges your correction, you will be prepared to show support for your work. What should you do if an author ignores your correct work and insists on using an incorrect form? Give in. The person who signs the document should have the final decision on its contents.

6. **Develop a system.** As you make corrections, use a code or system to remind yourself which citations have been checked and which remain to be corrected. Use checks, asterisks, colored pens, colored adhesive flags, or any other method that works for you. Then if your work is interrupted and you later need to return to the project, you can readily determine where you need to start.

7. **Work smart.** As you correct citations, you will undoubtedly notice that there are "holes" in the document, such as missing dates or missing pages of quotes. Rather than immediately filling in each gap as you come across it, mark each gap with a colored highlighter or adhesive flag. Later, you can either go to the law library or go online and locate all of the missing information in one efficient step rather than attempting a piecemeal approach. Use Lexis or Westlaw to help you verify the accuracy of case names,

pages, quotations, dates, and so forth. Similarly, if cite-checking for another, ask if the person has copies of the cases and other authorities cited in the brief. If so, sections of the cases may already be highlighted, allowing you to easily check the accuracy of quotations and other items.

8. **Be thorough.** Check all citations in the document. Ignore the temptation to focus on the argument section of a brief. Start at page one and look for every citation in the document, including those in the table of authorities, in footnotes, and any citations in any appendices.

9. **Be consistent.** If the author has been underscoring case names, ensure that book titles and citation signals such as id. and supra are likewise underscored. Conversely, if case names have been italicized, italicize book titles and signals

10. **Check the signals.** Citation signals such as *id.* tell a reader that a previously given citation supports a later statement. If you see signals such as *id.* and *supra,* check to ensure they match up with a previous citation. Why would they not? On many occasions an author may omit, insert, or move a section of a brief, forgetting that following signals may then be left hanging without a previous reference.

Practice Tips

✓ To ensure quick access to court rules, use the Internet site MegaLaw (http://www.megalaw.com), and bookmark the sites for the courts to which your office or firm routinely submits documents.

✓ Use standard proofreaders' marks when making corrections on a document. Some of the most frequently used marks are as follows:

#	Insert a space
⌒	Close up
∧	Insert
stet	Let the original text stand
ϒ	Delete text

✓ Images and examples of proofreaders' marks can be found at the following website: http://www.utexas.edu/visualguidelines/proofreaders.html.

Practice Tips

✓ Professor Peter W. Martin of Cornell University Law School has published an online guide to citation form entitled *Introduction to Basic Legal Citation* (rev. 2007). The guide provides information on the purpose of legal citations, examples for nearly all citation formats, and a table of state-specific citations, providing examples for cases, statutes, and regulations for all 50 states and the District of Columbia.

✓ The website address is as follows: http://www.law.cornell.edu/citation/.

✓ Consider "bookmarking" this valuable site as one of your favorite sites. Use it as a "backup" or to confirm the accuracy of your citations.

✓ Caveat: Although this site is excellent and provides great examples, always use *The Bluebook* as the final authority. Nevertheless, this website will provide you with a wealth of valuable information and numerous examples of citation form.

2 The Bluebook Trap: Typeface Conventions

Guiding Principle: Practitioners should be wary of most of the examples given in The Bluebook *other than those in the Bluepages (pages 3-24). While the words in the examples are in the right order, the presentation style is inappropriate for practitioners in that large and small capitals are used. According to* The Bluebook, *practitioners do not use large and small capitals and must convert any large and small capital styles to ordinary roman typeface.*

■ The Problem

Examine the inside front cover of *The Bluebook*, left-hand side, approximately halfway down the page. Note the reference to the following state constitution:

N.M. Const. art. IV, § 7.

Now examine the inside back cover of *The Bluebook* in the same location. Examine the reference to the same constitution:

N.M. Const. art. IV, § 7.

Can you tell the difference in the style in which the same source is presented?

11

Note that in the first example, the capital letters "N," "M," and the "C" in "CONST." are all slightly larger than the remaining capital letters in the word "CONST." while in the second example on the inside back cover the presentation shows only an initial capital letter.

What is going on? How can both be correct? Return to your copy of *The Bluebook*. Note the heading on the inside front cover: Quick Reference: Law Review Footnotes. Compare this with the heading on the inside back cover: Quick Reference: Court Documents and Legal Memoranda.

You are now ready to tackle perhaps the single most confusing thing about *The Bluebook*. Nearly all of the examples given in its white pages are for use in law review footnotes rather than for use by practitioners.

The Bluebook Approach

The Bluebook was originally developed solely for citations appearing in scholarly and academic articles appearing in law school publications, namely law journals or "law reviews." Only later was it adopted for general use by "practitioners," those people functioning in the "real world" of law practice. At the time *The Bluebook* was created, law review articles were generally typeset by professional printers who were able to use a format consisting of large and small capitals in which the first letter of a major word was displayed in a larger size capital letter than other letters in the word (for example, TRUSTS AND ESTATES).

Practitioners' Approach

Because practitioners used typewriters to prepare briefs and documents rather than having them typeset by printers, they could not reproduce the large and small capital presentation dictated by *The Bluebook,* and as a result, practitioners began converting the large and small capital formats shown in *The Bluebook* to a simpler style, generally referred to as "ordinary roman type" (for example, Trusts and Estates). Ordinary roman type is the typeface most often used in books, newspapers, and magazines. Popular roman font styles include Times New Roman and Garamond.

■ A Dual System of Citation

A twofold citation system thus developed with law reviews showing citations for state statutes, constitutions, book titles and authors, and periodical names in large and small capitals and practitioners showing those same citations in the simpler form, because practitioners were incapable at that time of producing large and small capitals on standard office typewriters.

Unfortunately, the dual system is generally not explained well (or even at all) to law or paralegal students or to those word processors who prepare briefs and other documents for practitioners. Many law students exit law school believing citations should be displayed in large and small capital letters only to discover that they must learn to convert most of the examples found in *The Bluebook* in order to comport with the style used by practitioners.

You may wonder why the dual system persists when, with today's word processors, it is easily possible for practitioners to use the large and small capital format. Such would result in a truly "uniform" system of citation with both law students and real-world practitioners presenting all citations in the same style. There is no good answer to this question. The dual system has persisted long after any need for it compels its use.

There are some other differences in the manner in which citations are presented in law review footnotes and in practitioners' documents. For example, return to the inside front and back covers of *The Bluebook* and note that in law review footnotes, full case names and book titles are not italicized or underscored while they are italicized or underscored by practitioners. Other differences will be discussed later. For now, it is enough for you to know that court documents and legal memoranda never use large and small capitals.

■ *The Bluebook's* Advice (Rule 2; B13)

The Bluebook itself makes only passing references to the confusing and seldom understood rule requiring differing presentation styles when one is preparing a law review article and when one is preparing a court document.

As discussed previously, the inside front and back covers of *The Bluebook* note that there is a difference in the typeface used in law review footnotes and that used by practitioners. Similarly, Rule 2 of *The Bluebook*, entitled Typefaces for Law Reviews, mentions the distinction; however, it merely instructs practitioners to assume the affirmative duty of substituting the typeface conventions found in the first section of *The Bluebook*, the Bluepages (a mere 21 pages), for those found in the remainder of *The Bluebook* (approximately 350 pages). Rule B13 states simply that "[l]arge and small caps are never used [by practitioners]." Thus, practitioners are primarily left to their own devices to figure out that most of *The Bluebook* is not for them. They will have to convert every instance of LARGE AND SMALL CAPITALS to a simpler style, namely ordinary roman type.

Lesson: If you are a practitioner, never use LARGE AND SMALL CAPITALS. In every instance in which you see such a presentation style in The Bluebook, *immediately convert it to the simpler style used by practitioners.*

If you have trouble remembering this rule, as you see examples throughout *The Bluebook,* ask yourself: Could I reproduce this presentation on an old-fashioned typewriter? If the answer is "no," it is a signal that the presentation was meant for printers who could manually typeset law review articles, not for practitioners.

Exercise for Chapter 2

The following are examples found in The Bluebook. *Correct them for use by practitioners.*

1. MODEL BUS. CORP. ACT § 57 (1979).

_____

2. U.S. CONST. art. IV, § 1.

_____

3. N.Y. BUS. CORP. LAW § 717 (McKinney 2003).

_____

4. BLACK'S LAW DICTIONARY 712 (7th ed. 1999).

_____

5. David Rudovsky, *Police Abuse: Can the Violence Be Contained?,* 27 HARV. C.R.-C.L. L. REV. 465, 500 (1992).

_____

6. H.R. REP. NO. 99-253, pt. 1, at 54 (1985).

---

7. FED. R. CIV. P. 11.

---

3 Citation Form for Cases

Introduction

There are several important rules to know about cases, primarily rules dealing with case names, rules relating to citation form for state and federal court cases, and related rules about abbreviations and spacing in case citations.

The required elements of a full case citation are as follows:

- The name of the case
- A reference to the published source where the case can be located
- Parenthetical information consisting of the year of decision and an identification of the court that issued the decision (if such is not apparent from the name of the set itself)
- Subsequent history of the case (if any)

Case Names (Rule 10.2; B5.1.1)

The rules relating to case names are discussed in *Bluebook* Rule 10.2 and Bluepages B5.1.1. Some of the more critical rules are as follows:

- Case names may be <u>underscored</u> or *italicized*. Some writers have a strong preference for one approach rather than another. It is possible that older practitioners who began careers before the advent of computers prefer underscoring because the typewriters on which they prepared their documents were not capable of any other style while younger practitioners may prefer italicizing because they are familiar with word processors that are capable of italicizing. Either approach is acceptable. Be consistent.

- When underscoring, underscore the entire case name using a solid unbroken line, including the "v." (B5.1.1) and any procedural phrase such as "In re."
- The "v." in a case citation is always a lowercase letter followed by a period.
- If the case names ends with an abbreviated word such as "Inc." or "Corp.," underscore or italicize the period in the abbreviation.
- Follow case names with a comma, which is neither underscored nor italicized.
- Give last names only of the parties in the case. Omit first names or initials, although always reproduce a business name scrupulously even if its name includes a person's name, as in *Carr v. Perry Ellis Co.*
- If there are multiple plaintiffs and defendants, list only the first plaintiff and the first defendant. Drop all other parties from the citation, and do not indicate that there are multiple parties by using an expression such as "et al.," a phrase meaning "and others."
- Do not identify the status of a party by including a term such as "plaintiff," "trustee," or "executor."
- Generally omit prepositional phrases of location (thus, the citation *Brown v. Board of Education* is correct while *Brown v. Board of Education of Topeka, Kansas* is not).
- Criminal cases from your state will be titled *State v. Lee, People v. Lee,* or *Commonwealth v. Lee* (if the case originates in the Commonwealth of Kentucky, Massachusetts, Pennsylvania, or Virginia). When the criminal case leaves your jurisdiction and goes to the U.S. Supreme Court on appeal, its name will change to *Arizona v. Lee* or *Pennsylvania v. Lee,* probably to facilitate indexing of case names.
- If the case name includes two business designations, such as both "Inc." and "Co.," retain the first and strike the second.
- Do not abbreviate "United States" in a case name if it is the entire name of a party.

Practice Tip

✓ Learn about cases from their names. The indication "v." in a case name indicates an adversarial matter. The indication "In re" in a case name usually indicates a nonadversarial matter, such as a bankruptcy, probate, or disbarment. It may also refer to large multidistrict litigation cases involving numerous parties, such as *In re Vitamin Antitrust Litigation* or *In re Teflon Products Liability Litigation.*

● If one of the parties is commonly referred to in spoken language by its initials rather than its full name (FBI, CIA, SEC), you may use that abbreviation and not include any periods (thus, *NLRB* is preferred while *N.L.R.B.* is not) (Rule 6.1(b)).

■ Abbreviations in Case Names
(Rule 10.2.1(c); B5.3 Table T.6)

You may have already noticed that many case names are lengthy. What words can you abbreviate in a citation to save space? The answer depends on how the citation is presented to the reader.

Note that Rule 10.2.1(c) states that when case names appear in textual sentences, you may abbreviate only widely known acronyms (such as FBI and FCC) and the following eight well-known abbreviations: &, Ass'n, Bros., Co., Corp., Inc., Ltd., and No.

Now examine Table T.6 of *The Bluebook*, which tells you that you always abbreviate any of the more than 160 words listed, including words such as "Liab.," "Distrib.," and "Hous." Such words are to be abbreviated even if they are the first or only word in a case name. How can these two statements possibly be reconciled?

Consider the way in which legal writers make arguments. Most commonly, they will make a statement about the law in a declaratory sentence ending with a period and then follow that statement with a citation. To avoid a rigid and rote approach, however, writers will often interweave citations into the middle of sentences. Which words can be abbreviated depends on which of these two styles is selected. The two governing rules are as follows:

- If your citation appears as part of a textual sentence (meaning that the citation is needed to make sense of the sentence), you should not distract your reader with odd-looking abbreviations. Thus, you may only abbreviate widely known acronyms (such as FBI and CIA) and the highly familiar eight words identified previously (such as "Inc." and "Co.").
- If, on the other hand, your citation stands alone as its own statement in support of (or in contradiction to) a previous declaration, unusual abbreviations will not distract the reader, and you must thus use any of the more than 160 words listed in Table T.6 (such as "Pub." and "Tech.").

Examples

- Punitive damages are recoverable in fraud actions. *W. Util. & Transp. Co. v. Lakewood Ref. Inc.*, 450 U.S. 24, 27 (1990).
- Although punitive damages are recoverable for fraud according to *Western Utility & Transportation Co. v. Lakewood Refining Inc.*, 450 U.S. 24, 27 (1990), those damages must bear a rational relationship to actual damages, *Peterson Indem. Co. v. Int'l Lab. Co.*, 451 U.S. 191, 199 (1992).

How will you remember this difficult rule? Consider that you already know this rule because you see it in practice everyday. You seldom, if ever, see abbreviations in novels or magazine articles, even commonly used abbreviations such as "St." for "Street." Abbreviations typically end with periods and are thus jarring and distracting to readers if they appear in the middle of sentences. Thus, remember that if your citation is part of a sentence, don't distract your reader with odd-looking abbreviations; however, if your citation "stands alone," the reader doesn't need it to make sense of the sentence and will not be bothered by abbreviated words.

Practice Tips

✓ Write across the top of Table T.6 of your *Bluebook* the note "For Stand-Alone Citations Only" to remind you that the listed abbreviations can only be used when your citation stands alone as its own sentence.

✓ Abbreviate states and other geographical units as shown in Table T.10.

✓ Unless otherwise indicated in Table T.6, to pluralize an abbreviation just add an "s" to the abbreviation (before the period), such as changing "Hosp." to "Hosps."

✓ If one of the eight well-known words (such as Co. or Inc.) begins a party's name it cannot be abbreviated.

Until 2000, *The Bluebook* prohibited abbreviating the first word in a plaintiff's or defendant's name. The current rule requires you to abbreviate any of the words in Table T.6, even if that word is the first word in a party's name (in a "stand alone" citation) as shown in the first example above. Many law firms and practitioners dislike this rule and continue to follow the prior rule by never abbreviating the first word in a party's name.

■ State Court Cases (Rule 10.3; B5.1.3)

Background

To master citation form for state court cases, one must understand how cases are published. Cases are published either officially (meaning their publication is mandated by a statute) or unofficially (meaning they are published without such authority). Years ago, nearly all states mandated that their appellate court cases that advanced legal theory be published. The sets of books that collected these decisions were called *reports* and generally were indicated by a state abbreviation ("Minn." for cases from Minnesota, "Cal." for cases from California, and so forth). Because publication of these sets was government approved, they were called "official."

Because what courts decide is a matter of public record and is not subject to copyright protection, anyone can copy cases that are already published, print the cases, and bind them, perhaps adding some editorial features. Such a set is *unofficial,* meaning its publication is not authorized by the state legislature but is rather the result of some independent act of a third party.

Such action was undertaken by two brothers named John and Horatio West in the late 1800s. They republished cases that had already been published officially, grouped them together in various geographical units, and began selling the sets to practitioners. The company, now Thomson/ West (hereinafter "West") thus produces the *North Western Reporter*, which publishes cases from North Dakota, South Dakota, Nebraska, Minnesota, Iowa, Wisconsin, and Michigan. A Wisconsin case that appears in the *North Western Reporter* is the same as the Wisconsin case published in the official *Wisconsin Reports*, although certain editorial enhancements may vary from set to set. Thus, the case *Brown v. Whitney* might be located at 432 Wis. 2d 13 and at 209 N.W.2d 421. The two citations are called *parallel* citations.

West also produces other sets of books that arrange cases published in certain geographical units. (See Figure 3-1.)

After West created the seven geographical or regional units, it decided that certain states produced so much case law they should have their own sets of books, and so it created the *California Reporter*, the *New York Supplement*, and *Illinois Decisions* (for cases from those states). Thus, for example, a newer California Supreme Court case will have three parallel citations: a reference to its publication in the official *California Reports*, a reference to its publication in the *Pacific Reporter*, and a reference to its publication in the more newly created specialized set, *California Reporter*.

Some practitioners might prefer to buy the official *California Reports* while others might prefer to obtain access to cases from surrounding states by purchasing the *Pacific Reporter*.

Practice Tip

✓ A color-coded map showing the grouping of states in West's National Reporter System can be found at the website of the University of Denver Sturm College of Law at: http://www.law.du.edu/daustin/alr/reportermap.pdf.

Citation Form

For nearly 70 years, *The Bluebook* required that practitioners provide all parallel citations when citing state court cases, reasoning that the author could not possibly know what set of books the reader had in his or her law office or judge's chambers, and thus, authors should provide all citations to enable a reader to locate easily any cited case. Writers were required to give the official citation first, followed by a comma and then the unofficial citation.

Atlantic Reporter *(A., A.2d)*	Connecticut, Delaware, Maine, Maryland, New Hampshire, New Jersey, Pennsylvania, Rhode Island, Vermont, Washington, D.C.
North Eastern Reporter *(N.E, N.E.2d)*	Illinois, Indiana, Massachusetts, New York, Ohio
South Eastern Reporter *(S.E., S.E.2d)*	Georgia, North Carolina, South Carolina, Virginia, West Virginia
Southern Reporter *(So., So. 2d)*	Alabama, Florida, Louisiana, Mississippi
North Western Reporter *(N.W., N.W.2d)*	Iowa, Michigan, Minnesota, Nebraska, North Dakota, South Dakota, Wisconsin
South Western Reporter *(S.W., S.W.2d, S.W.3d)*	Arkansas, Kentucky, Missouri, Tennessee, Texas
Pacific Reporter *(P., P.2d, P.3d)*	Alaska, Arizona, California, Colorado, Hawaii, Idaho, Kansas, Montana, Nevada, New Mexico, Oklahoma, Oregon, Utah, Washington, Wyoming

Figure 3-1   West's National Reporter System for State Court Cases

Although the rule relating to citation of state court cases has been revised a bit since 1991, the current rule (from the Eighteenth Edition of *The Bluebook*) is as follows:

- If court rules require parallel citations, you must give them (giving the official citation first, followed by the unofficial citation(s)).
- Unless court rules require parallel citations, cite solely to the regional reporter (for example, P.2d or N.W.2d), and give a reference to the state, the deciding court, and the year of decision parenthetically. (See B5.1.3 and Rules 10.3.1 and 10.4.)

Thus, if you are citing a Virginia case in a document sent to a court that requires parallel citations, you must give them (listing the official citation first and the unofficial second). If you are citing the same case in any other instance, give only the regional citation. As always, if local rules exist regarding citation form, they supersede *The Bluebook* rules.

How will you know which is the official citation that must be placed first and which is the unofficial citation that must be placed second? The official citation includes an abbreviation for the state (such as "Cal." or "Ga."), while the unofficial citation is generally a regional abbreviation (such as "A." for "Atlantic," "S.E." for South Eastern, and so forth). The courts of each state are listed in *The Bluebook* in Table T.1 from highest court to lowest court.

Although the state-by-state summary in Table T.1 provides instruction on citing state court cases, the information in Table T.1 is directed to citation form for law review footnotes. Practitioners should thus follow the format and examples given in the Bluepages section of *The Bluebook*.

Remember that cases from California, Illinois, and New York may have three parallel citations, and you must order the citation as outlined in Table T.1 in *The Bluebook*.

Examples

- *Samson Corp. v. Bailey*, 302 Va. 118, 671 S.E.2d 909 (1990). This form is used when a court rule requires parallel citations.
- *Samson Corp. v. Bailey*, 671 S.E.2d 909 (Va. 1990). This form is used in any instance other than when a court rule requires parallel citations.

Parentheticals for State Court Cases
(Rule 10.4(b); B5.1.3)

Note the parenthetical given in the preceding second example. Without the indication of "Va." in the parenthetical, the reader would have no idea which of the five states in the *South Eastern Reporter* issued the decision. The reader must be given this critical piece of information.

If the parenthetical merely gives the abbreviation for the state (such as "Cal." or "Va."), it is an indication that the case is from the highest court in that state. (Rule 10.4(b)). If the case was decided by a court other than the highest court, you must indicate such in the parenthetical, generally by providing the abbreviation "Ct. App." For example, the citation *State v. Bowie*, 429 P.2d 136 (Cal. Ct. App. 1958), indicates the case is from the intermediate appellate court in California while the citation *Franks v. Park*, 436 P.2d 102 (Cal. 1992), indicates the case was decided by the highest court in California, the California Supreme Court. Similarly, "(Kan. 1996)" indicates a 1996 decision of the Kansas Supreme Court, while "(Kan. Ct. App. 1996)" indicates a 1996 decision of the Kansas Court of Appeals. When the deciding state is clear from the name of the official reporter set (as it is in "Cal." or "Kan."), it is not needed in a parenthetical (see the preceding first example). Similarly, you do not need to indicate the name of a court if the deciding court is the highest one in that state. Do not indicate the department or district that decided a case unless that information is particularly relevant. Note that there is a space before the parenthetical is opened.

Remember that local rules always supersede *Bluebook* rules. For example, although *The Bluebook* clearly states that there is no need to indicate which state department or court district decided a case unless it is of particular relevance (Rule 10.4), local Florida rules require such. Similarly, although *The Bluebook* shows the abbreviation for the set *Washington Reports* as "Wash.," local court rules require that the set be shown as "Wn." Most local rules can be accessed through MegaLaw at http://www.megalaw.com.

In a few states, including Arizona, Hawaii, Idaho, New Mexico, South Carolina, and Wisconsin, cases from the state supreme court and from the state court of appeals are published in one set. For example, *Idaho Reports* now publishes decisions from the Idaho Supreme Court and from the Idaho Court of Appeals. Because the name of the set, *Idaho Reports,* does not tell which court decided the case, additional information is required in the parenthetical, when referring to appellate court cases, as follows: *Bell v. Hall,* 204 Idaho 14, 611 P.2d 84 (Ct. App. 1990). Note that no reference to "Idaho" is given in the parenthetical because the reader can easily tell which state decided the case.

Some states, such as Alabama and Tennessee, have separate courts of criminal appeals. Citations to those cases would be given as follows:

State v. Harris, 82 Tenn. Crim. App. 141, 203 S.W.2d 18 (1968)
(if a court rule requires parallel citations).

or

State v. Harris, 203 S.W.2d 18 (Tenn. Crim. App. 1968).

Finally, some states (Maine, Montana, Nevada, New Hampshire, Rhode Island, South Dakota, Vermont, West Virginia, and Wyoming) have no intermediate appellate courts. In those states, all citations are to the state supreme court.

How will you know which states have no intermediate appellate court? Review Table T.1 of *The Bluebook* (for example, see page 218 of *The Bluebook* which lists only a supreme court for New Hampshire), or access the website for the National Center for State Courts (http://www.ncsconline.org), which provides court structure charts for each state.

Discontinuation of Some Official Reports

Because West's unofficial reporters became so successful, and many practitioners preferred the West reporters over their own official state reports, a number of states (generally the less populous ones) ceased publishing officially. For cases from these states, you will only be able to cite to West's unofficial regional reporter (and then provide the appropriate parenthetical information). You will not be able to include an official citation because one does not exist after the date official publication ceased. For cases decided prior to the date official publication ceased, follow the normal citation rules for state court cases discussed previously (namely, give parallel citations only when local rules require).

How can one determine if a state has discontinued official publication? Table T.1 of *The Bluebook* provides the answer. For example, note that the entry for West Virginia on page 238 states that the *West Virginia Reports* covers cases from "1864-date" while page 239 indicates that the *Wyoming Reports* covers cases from "1870-1959." Such is an indication that West Virginia is still publishing officially while Wyoming ceased official publication in 1959. Thus, for any case decided in Wyoming after 1959, the citation form is as follows:

> *Wong v. Harris,* 590 P.2d 118 (Wyo. 1985). (Note: For cases from Wyoming prior to 1959, you may need to include both parallel citations, namely to Wyo. and to P. or P.2d, if local rules require parallel citations.)

See the Appendix, Examples of State Cases and Statutes, for sample citations for all states and the District of Columbia. See Figure 3-2 for a table of discontinued official state court reports.

Public Domain Citations
(Rule 10.3.3)

Both the American Bar Association (ABA) and the American Association of Law Libraries (AALL) have recommended that courts adopt a public domain or uniform or universal citation system to allow a citation system for cases that would be equally effective whether the cases are found in conventional print form or in electronic form. The system is also referred to as "vendor neutral" or "medium neutral," meaning that the citation will look the same whether the case is found in a printed book, in CD-ROM form, on Lexis or Westlaw, or on the Internet.

State	Year of Discontinuation	State	Year of Discontinuation
Alabama	1976	Minnesota	1977
Alaska	Never published cases officially	Mississippi	1966
Colorado	1980	Missouri	1956
Delaware	1966	North Dakota	1953
District of Columbia	1941	Oklahoma	1953
Florida	1948	Rhode Island	1980
Indiana	1981	South Dakota	1976
Iowa	1968	Tennessee	1972
Kentucky	1951	Texas	1962
Louisiana	1971	Utah	1974
Maine	1965	Wyoming	1959

Figure 3-2   Table of Discontinued Official State Court Reports

Rule 10.3.3, in discussing parallel citations for state court cases, states that if a state court decision is available through an official public domain citation, this citation must be given, and a citation to the relevant regional reporter (A., P., S.W., and so forth) must be provided as well. To assist readers, the regional citation is included because it is so well recognized. Thus, the public domain citation really only replaces the official citation because the regional citation continues to exist. The citation should include the case name, year of decision, the state's two-character postal code (found in Table T.1), abbreviation of court issuing the decision (unless the court is the state's highest court), sequential number of the decision, paragraph number (when one refers to specific material in the case), and the regional reporter citation (if available). If the decision is unpublished, place a capital "U" after the sequential number. Note that public domain formats are adopted for use after specified dates. (See Table T.1.) Citation form for cases before the effective date should follow the format described earlier for state court cases.

Example

Wade v. Lee, 1997 ME 44, ¶ 15, 401 A.2d 909, 914.

At this time, Louisiana, Maine, Mississippi, Montana, New Mexico, North Dakota, Ohio, Oklahoma, Pennsylvania (for superior court cases), South Dakota, Utah, Vermont, Wisconsin, and Wyoming have adopted public domain citation systems, and other states may be considering doing so. When citing to cases from these states, check state and local rules and the examples shown in Table T.1 of *The Bluebook*. In the absence of instruction, follow *The Bluebook*. Additional information on this topic is found in Chapter 6.

Practice Tip

✓ Be particularly careful when citing to cases from states that have adopted uniform or public domain citation formats. Presentation styles vary significantly. Some states continue to require that case names be italicized or underscored; others do not. Some states follow *The Bluebook* approach and show a space between a paragraph symbol and its number (as in ¶ 14) and others do not (as in ¶14). Additional information about this topic, and information about particular state formats and rules can be found at the website for the ABA Legal Technology Resource Center at http://www.abanet.org/tech/ltrc/research/citation/home.html.

■ Federal Court Cases (B5.1.3; Table T.1)

Background

To understand how to cite cases from our federal courts, you must first have a basic understanding of our federal court structure. The trial courts in our federal system are called "district courts." They may handle a wide variety of cases, from bank robbery to free speech to copyright cases. There are more than 90 district courts for the United States and its territories. Each state has at least one district court, and if a state has a heavy caseload and/or comprises a significant geographic area, it may have more than one district court. Thus, New Jersey has one district court while California has four district courts. (See Figure 3-3, which identifies district courts and U.S. courts of appeals.)

Litigants who lose a case in the district court can appeal an adverse decision to our intermediate federal courts of appeals. The United States is divided into 13 areas, often called "circuits," with various states being grouped into a circuit. Thus, New York, Connecticut, and Vermont are in the Second Circuit, and most western states are in the Ninth Circuit. We have 11 numbered circuits, one for the District of Columbia, and one called the "Federal Circuit" that primarily handles patent matters and appeals from administrative agencies. (See Figure 3-4 for a map of the thirteen federal judicial circuits.)

A litigant who loses in a federal circuit may then attempt to appeal the adverse decision to the U.S. Supreme Court. However, the Supreme Court generally has the discretion to determine which cases it accepts for review and which it does not. When it accepts a case for review it "grants certiorari" (certiorari is a Latin word meaning "to be informed of"). If it refuses to take the case, as it does more than 95 percent of the time, it "denies certiorari."

While there are federal courts other than those discussed here (tax courts, military justice courts, and bankruptcy courts, for example), this text addresses citation form for the most commonly encountered federal cases. Use Table T.1 of *The Bluebook* to determine citation form for cases from federal courts other than those discussed herein.

Citation of Federal Court Cases (B5.1.3; Table T.1)

District Court Cases

Ordinarily, trial court cases in this country are not published. There are simply too many of them. West, however, decided to create a set of books to publish some cases from the district courts (the trial courts in our federal system) because important federal or constitutional issues may be raised in such cases. The set West created is called the *Federal Supplement* (abbreviated as "F. Supp." or F. Supp. 2d"). It is unofficial, and there are no parallel citations for cases from the federal district courts. Every citation, however, must include a reference to the specific deciding court, so include the district court information in the parenthetical with the date.

State	District Courts	Circuit
Alabama	M.D. Ala. N.D. Ala. S.D. Ala.	11th Cir.
Alaska	D. Alaska	9th Cir.
Arizona	D. Ariz.	9th Cir.
Arkansas	E.D. Ark. W.D. Ark.	8th Cir.
California	C.D. Cal. E.D. Cal. N.D. Cal. S.D. Cal.	9th Cir.
Colorado	D. Colo.	10th Cir.
Connecticut	D. Conn.	2d Cir.
Delaware	D. Del.	3d Cir.
District of Columbia	D.D.C.	D.C. Cir
Florida	M.D. Fla. N.D. Fla. S.D. Fla.	11th Cir.
Georgia	M.D. Ga. N.D. Ga. S.D. Ga.	11th Cir.
Hawaii	D. Haw.	9th Cir.
Idaho	D. Idaho	9th Cir.
Illinois	C.D. Ill. N.D. Ill. S.D. Ill.	7th Cir.
Indiana	N.D. Ind. S.D. Ind.	7th Cir.
Iowa	N.D. Iowa S.D. Iowa	8th Cir.
Kansas	D. Kan.	10th Cir.
Kentucky	E.D. Ky. W.D. Ky.	6th Cir.
Louisiana	E.D. La. M.D. La. W.D. La.	5th Cir.
Maine	D. Me.	1st Cir.
Maryland	D. Md.	4th Cir.
Massachusetts	D. Mass.	1st Cir.
Michigan	E.D. Mich. W.D. Mich.	6th Cir.
Minnesota	D. Minn.	8th Cir.
Mississippi	N.D. Miss. S.D. Miss.	5th Cir.
Missouri	E.D. Mo. W.D. Mo.	8th Cir.

Figure 3-3 District Courts and U.S. Courts of Appeal

State	District Court	Court of Appeal
Montana	D. Mont.	9th Cir.
Nebraska	D. Neb.	8th Cir.
Nevada	D. Nev.	9th Cir.
New Hampshire	D.N.H.	1st Cir.
New Jersey	D.N.J.	3d Cir.
New Mexico	D.N.M.	10th Cir.
New York	E.D.N.Y.	2d Cir.
	N.D.N.Y.	
	S.D.N.Y.	
	W.D.N.Y.	
North Carolina	E.D.N.C.	4th Cir.
	M.D.N.C.	
	W.D.N.C.	
North Dakota	D.N.D.	8th Cir.
Ohio	N.D. Ohio	6th Cir.
	S.D. Ohio	
Oklahoma	E.D. Okla.	10th Cir.
	N.D. Okla.	
	W.D. Okla.	
Oregon	D. Or.	9th Cir.
Pennsylvania	E.D. Pa.	3d Cir.
	M.D. Pa.	
	W.D. Pa.	
Rhode Island	D.R.I.	1st Cir.
South Carolina	D.S.C.	4th Cir.
South Dakota	D.S.D.	8th Cir.
Tennessee	E.D. Tenn.	6th Cir.
	M.D. Tenn.	
	W.D. Tenn.	
Texas	E.D. Tex.	5th Cir.
	N.D. Tex.	
	S.D. Tex.	
	W.D. Tex.	
Utah	D. Utah	10th Cir.
Vermont	D. Vt.	2d Cir.
Virginia	E.D. Va.	4th Cir.
	W.D. Va.	
Washington	E.D. Wash.	9th Cir.
	W.D. Wash.	
West Virginia	N.D.W. Va.	4th Cir.
	S.D.W. Va.	
Wisconsin	E.D. Wis.	7th Cir.
	W.D. Wis.	
Wyoming	D. Wyo.	10th Cir.
U.S. Court of Appeals for the Federal Circuit	Fed. Cir.	
U.S. Court of Appeals for the District of Columbia	D.C. Cir.	

Figure 3-3 District Courts and U.S. Courts of Appeal (*continued*)

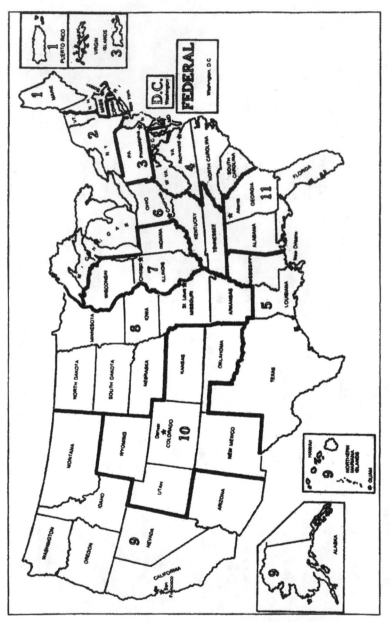

Figure 3-4 The Thirteen Federal Judicial Circuits. *See* 28 U.S.C.A. § 41

Examples

Corey v. Shea, 889 F. Supp. 16 (E.D. Va. 1987).
Joshua Tree Ltd. v. Baker, 10 F. Supp. 2d 190 (S.D.N.Y. 1999).

Courts of Appeals Cases

At present, there is only one set of books that reports published cases from the intermediate courts of appeals: *Federal Reporter* (abbreviated as "F.," "F.2d," or "F.3d"), an unofficial set published by West. Thus, you need not worry about parallel citations for cases from the intermediate courts of appeals. Every citation, however, must include a reference to the specific deciding court, so always include the circuit information in the parenthetical with the date.

Examples

Ray v. Libby Co., 789 F.2d 118 (2d Cir. 1994).
Atl. Mgmt. Co. v. Moe, 15 F.3d 931 (Fed. Cir. 1998).

A newly created set published by West, *Federal Appendix*, publishes decisions since 2001 from most of the intermediate courts of appeal that have not been designated for publication. Federal courts now allow citation to unpublished cases, but always check your local rules relating to citing such cases.

U.S. Supreme Court Cases

Cases from the U.S. Supreme Court are published in a variety of sources. They are published officially in a set called *United States Reports*, and they are published unofficially in three places: by West in a set called *Supreme Court Reporter*, by LexisNexis in a set called *Lawyers Edition* (or *Lawyers Edition, Second Series*), and in a weekly journal called *United States Law Week*. Additionally, U.S. Supreme Court cases can be located through Lexis, Westlaw, and on the Internet at the Court's website at http://www. supremecourtus.gov.

Although there are thus at least four parallel citations for U.S. Supreme Court cases, *The Bluebook* rule is direct: Cite to *United States Reports* (U.S.) if the case is published in that set. If not, cite to *Supreme Court Reporter*

Figure 3-5 provides a diagram of the federal court system.

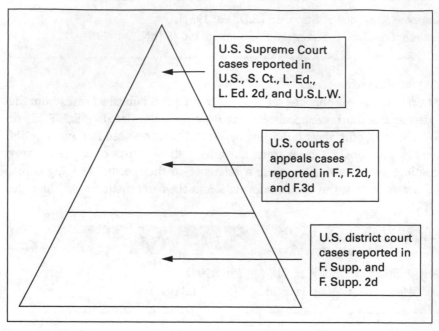

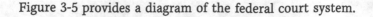

Figure 3-5 Federal Court System (excluding administrative and specialized courts)

(S. Ct.), *Lawyers Edition* (L. Ed. or L. Ed. 2d), or *United States Law Week* (U.S.L.W.) in that order of preference. Do not give a parallel citation.

If you are wondering why a case would not be published in the official *United States Reports*, remember that the set is official. It is published under government authority. The commercial publishers release volumes much more quickly. Thus, for newer cases, the official citation may not yet be available, requiring you to cite to one of the other sets.

Examples

Farley v. Galloway, 501 U.S. 699 (1998).
Hall v. Porter, 239 S. Ct. 993 (2007).

The second citation would be for a case not yet published in the official *United States Reports*.

Practice Tip

✓ Some practitioners use the form *Taylor v. Green*, _____ U.S. _____, 241 S. Ct. 90 (2007) for recent cases, presumably to indicate to a reader that while an official citation will eventually exist, it is not available yet, and thus the author is providing the reader with the "default" citation from the *Supreme Court Reporter*. Although this technique is commonly encountered in practice, there is no authority for it in *The Bluebook*. Check your firm or office practice.

Public Domain Citations

Although the ABA has recommended a public domain citation system for federal cases, such a system has not been mandated by any federal courts. The use of a public domain citation is optional in the Sixth Circuit (covering Kentucky Michigan, Ohio, and Tennessee). Most federal courts, however, adamantly oppose such citations. Thus, until further change is announced, follow *The Bluebook* and the examples herein. A public domain citation from the Sixth Circuit would be *Allen v. Gray*, 1999 FED App. 0184P (6th Cir.). (See example in Table T.1 of *The Bluebook*.) Further discussion of this topic is found in Chapter 6.

Practice Tip

✓ Color-coded maps of West's National Reporter System and the U.S. Courts of Appeal are available on the Internet. Bookmark the following websites so these maps are readily available to you.

    National Reporter System Map:
    http://www.law.du.edu/daustin/alr/reportermap.pdf
    U.S. Courts of Appeal Map:
    http://www.uscourts.gov/courtlinks/index.cfm

■ Subsequent and Prior History
(Rule 10.7, Table T.8)

Subsequent History

When you "Shepardize" or "KeyCite" a case to determine whether it is still good law, you will find the subsequent history and treatment of the case as later courts or cases have discussed it. According to *Bluebook* Rule 10.7, you are ethically obligated to give the entire subsequent history of a case. Nevertheless, omit the following subsequent history:

- Denials of certiorari or denials of similar discretionary appeals, unless your case is less than two years old or the denial is particularly relevant.
- History on remand (when a case is returned or remanded to a trial court by an appellate court to ensure the lower court complies with the appellate court's instructions), unless relevant.
- Denials of discretionary appeals, such as rehearings (when a disappointed party requests that a court reconsider or rehear a case), unless relevant. Because rehearings are so often requested and seldom granted, generally omit this information.

Until the Sixteenth Edition of *The Bluebook* in 1996, one was always required to include a denial of certiorari. The Sixteenth, Seventeenth, and Eighteenth Editions of *The Bluebook* instruct writers to omit such denials unless the case is recent (less than two years old) or the denial is particularly relevant. Some practitioners object to the new rule, believing that the denial of certiorari sends a signal to a reader that a case is final and is, thus, always relevant. Determine if your firm or office has a policy regarding this matter.

How does one indicate subsequent history? When you Shepardize the case and find the subsequent history, consult Table T.8 of *The Bluebook* for the appropriate abbreviation and then cite as follows:

Examples

Young v. Barr Co., 45 F.3d 18 (D.C. Cir. 2006), *cert. denied,* 530 U.S. 166 (2007). (Note: If underscoring, use a solid unbroken line for cert. denied.)

Jacobs v. Nelson, 789 F. Supp. 16 (D.N.J. 1994), *rev'd,* 904 F.2d 18 (3d Cir. 1995).

Practice Tip

✓ If the date in the second parenthetical will be the same as that in the first, strike the date from the first parenthetical and retain it only in the second (Rule 10.5(d)) as follows:

Li v. Li, 44 F.3d 21 (9th Cir.), *aff'd*, 519 U.S. 901 (1998).

Prior History

Virtually all cases from the U.S. Supreme Court (and the highest courts in a state) have prior history because they were not originally decided by the Supreme Court but came to the Court from lower appellate courts. Are you required to give the prior history of such a case or other cases with prior history? No. Only give prior history if it is significant to the point you are making.

Practice Tips

✓ **Federal cases:** You never need to give parallel citations for federal cases. When citing to U.S. Supreme Court cases, cite only to U.S. (if the case is published in that set). Lower federal court cases have no parallel citations.

✓ **State cases:** Give a parallel citation only if a local rule requires such. Otherwise, cite to the regional reporter and then show the state and court of decision in the parenthetical with the year of decision (although you may omit the name of the court if the case is from the highest court in that jurisdiction). Remember that more than 20 states no longer publish their cases officially; for these states, it is no longer possible to include a parallel citation.

▮ Series of Court Reports

You may have noticed that some citations are to "F.," while others are to "F.2d" or "F.3d." Similarly, some citations are to "N.E." while others are to "N.E.2d." Why? As publishers publish cases in the court reports, the volume numbers of the sets keep increasing. Probably to ensure that the volume number does not become confusingly high, the publishers eventually stop publishing an initial set (such as F. or N.E.) and begin publishing a new series (such as F.2d or N.E.2d). Still other sets can have higher series numbers such as Cal. 4th. You do not need to know when the series numbers switch over. You need only know that any case in F.3d is newer than any case in F.2d, and likewise any case in F.2d is newer than any case in F.

Note that the abbreviation for "second" in legal citations is always "2d" (rather than the nonlegal abbreviation "2nd" that is commonly used). Similarly, the abbreviation for "third" in legal citations is always "3d" and not "3rd." Other abbreviations, such as those for 4th, 5th, and so forth are identical to those used in nonlegal writing.

Practice Tip

✓ You may have noticed that when you type ordinals such as "6th" or "4th" when referring to the Sixth or Fourth Circuit Courts of Appeal, your word processor may elevate the "th" to superscript form (as in "6th" or "4th"). *The Bluebook* flatly prohibits the use of superscripts (Rule 6.2(b)).

Incorrect: (8th Cir. 2004)
Correct: (8th Cir. 2004)

✓ You may disable this feature on your word processor by selecting "Tools," then "AutoCorrect," and then "AutoFormat As You Type." Uncheck the appropriate box relating to superscripts.

■ **Spacing in Citations** (Rule 6.1(a))

The following spacing rules apply to all citations, not merely cases. There are three spacing rules:

- If a single capital letter is followed by another single capital letter, close them up together with no spaces (for purposes of this rule, numerals and ordinals are treated as single capitals), and close up initials in personal names.

  A.2d   S.W.   U.S.   F.3d   N.W.2d   A.L.R.5th   J.C. Jones

- Multiple letter abbreviations (such as "Cal." and "Supp.") are preceded and followed by spaces.

Cal. App.   F. Supp. 2d   So. 2d   S. Ct.   D. Minn.   Fed. R. Civ. P.

- Be careful with the abbreviations for periodicals. The spacing rule requires you to determine if one or more of the capitals refers to the name of an institutional entity, such as a school. If so, set the capital or capitals referring to the entity apart from other single capitals. Because this rule is so confusing, you should simply consult Table T.13, which gives abbreviations for more than 700 periodicals, and mimic the spacing you see. (Note, however, that you must convert the large and small capitals to ordinary roman type.)

N.C. L. Rev.   N.M. L. Rev.

Exercise for Chapter 3

Correct the following citations. You may need to supply or create missing information. There may be more than one thing wrong with the citation.

Case Names

1. Tracy Singer versus A.M. Kimball

_____

2. T.N. Andrews, III, Vs. Blake Ellison, James Gray, and Leon Nelson

_____

3. Commonwealth of Virginia V. Talbot Chemical Department, a state court case (Assume the citation appears as a "stand-alone" citation.)

_____

4. USA v. Reynolds Building Federation Incorporated (Cite first assuming citation appears in a textual sentence, and then cite as a stand-alone citation.)

_____

5. Helen and Delia Parry versus Securities and Exchange Commission

State Court Cases

6. Forras v. Hecker, 309 Massachusetts 601 (Assume citation appears in a brief submitted to a court requiring parallel citations.)

7. Douglas v. Dixon, 201 Cal. 3rd 990, 89 California Reporter 14, 909 Pacific Reporter (Second Series) 292 (2003). (Assume the citation appears in a brief submitted to a court requiring parallel citations).

8. Douglas v. Dixon, 201 Cal. 3rd 990, 89 California Reporter 14, 909 Pacific Reporter (Second Series) 292 (2003). (Assume the citation appears in a brief submitted to a court that does not require parallel citations.)

9. Smithson v. Garcia, an Indiana Supreme Court case decided in 2000.

10. United States v. Nordic Village, Inc., a 2004 Indiana court of appeals case (Assume the citation appears as a stand-alone citation).

Federal Cases and Subsequent History

11. Jeffrey v. Cross Country Bank, 530 United States Reports 616, 214 Supreme Court Reporter 144, 210 Lawyers Edition, Second Series, 995 (2001).

12. Hornbuckle v. State Farm Lloyds, a 2006 Fifth Circuit case located at volume 385 of the Federal Reporter, Third Series, at page 538. (Assume certiorari was denied for this case by the United States Supreme Court in 2007).

13 Rains LLC v. Arco Products Co., 405 F. 3d 764 (2003). (Assume this case was affirmed by the United States Supreme Court in 2005).

14. Charter Company v. Riggs Bank of Washington, D.C., 23 Federal Supplement, Second Series, page 119.

15. Alvaro v. Gustin, a case from the Southern District of New York, decided in 2005 and reversed by the Second Circuit Court of Appeals in 2005.

Spacing

16. 38 Federal Reporter (Third Series) 107.

17. 402 New York Reports, Second Series, page 607.

18. Sullivan v. Sullivan, 526 United States Reports 111 (2003).

19. Aztec Inc. v. Zodiac Co., 206 West Virginia Reports 114, 761 South Eastern Reporter (Second Series) 877 (2002).

20. 47 New York University Law Review 26 (2000).

21. 27 South Carolina Law Review 207 (2001).

4 Citation Form for Statutes, Legislative Materials, Uniform Acts, Court Rules, and Constitutions

Statutes (Rule 12; B6)

Federal Statutes

Introduction

Federal statutes are published in three separate sources. They are published officially in a set called the *United States Code*, and they are published unofficially by West in a set called *United States Code Annotated* and by LexisNexis in a set called *United States Code Service*. The basic citation form is the same for each set.

A citation must include the following elements:

- Reference to the title within the set
- Reference to the abbreviated name of the set
- Citation to the relevant statutory section

- Parenthetical that includes a year and, if you cite to anything other than the official set, a reference to the publisher of the unofficial set (although practitioners nearly always omit the entire parenthetical)

Thus, a reference to "17 U.S.C. § 107 (2000)" directs a reader to title 17 of the *United States Code*, section 107. See Figure 4-1 for a listing of titles for federal statutes.

1. General Provisions
2. The Congress
3. The President
4. Flag and Seal, Seat of Government, and the States
5. Government Organization and Employees
6. Surety Bonds
7. Agriculture
8. Aliens and Nationality
9. Arbitration
10. Armed Forces
11. Bankruptcy
12. Banks and Banking
13. Census
14. Coast Guard
15. Commerce and Trade
16. Conservation
17. Copyrights
18. Crimes and Criminal Procedure
19. Customs Duties
20. Education
21. Food and Drugs
22. Foreign Relations and Intercourse
23. Highways
24. Hospitals and Asylums
25. Indians
26. Internal Revenue Code
27. Intoxicating Liquors
28. Judiciary and Judicial Procedure
29. Labor
30. Mineral Lands and Mining
31. Money and Finance
32. National Guard
33. Navigation and Navigable Waters
34. Navy (see Title 10, Armed Forces)
35. Patents
36. Patriotic Societies and Observances
37. Pay and Allowances of the Uniformed Services
38. Veterans' Benefits
39. Postal Service
40. Public Buildings, Property, and Works
41. Public Contracts
42. The Public Health and Welfare
43. Public Lands
44. Public Printing and Documents
45. Railroads
46. Shipping
47. Telegraphs, Telephones, and Radiotelegraphs
48. Territories and Insular Possessions
49. Transportation
50. War and National Defense

Figure 4-1 Titles of United States Code

Examples

35 U.S.C. § 101 (2000).
35 U.S.C.A. § 101 (West 1999).
35 U.S.C.S. § 101 (LexisNexis 2003).

State Statutes

Most of the 50 states and the District of Columbia refer to their statutes merely by title, chapter, and section numbers. Consult Table T.1 for the blueprint for each state jurisdiction (but remember to convert the typeface from large and small capitals to ordinary roman type).

Examples

Colo. Rev. Stat. Ann. § 7-101-101 (West 19xx).
Neb. Rev. Stat. Ann. § 13-201 (LexisNexis 19xx).
Ohio Rev. Code Ann. § 1701.01 (West 19xx).

Some states, however, generally the more populous ones (including California, Maryland, New York, and Texas) have so many statutes that they are categorized into separately named titles. Once again, follow the format provided for each state in Table T.1.

Examples

Cal. Evid. Code § 52 (West 19xx).
Md. Code Ann., Educ. § 16-148 (West 19xx).
N.Y. Bus. Corp. Law § 694 (McKinney 19xx).

Miscellaneous Information

Year

According to *Bluebook* Rule 12.3.2, the year that is placed in the parenthetical is not the year the statute was enacted but rather the year found on the spine of the book, the year appearing on the title page, or the latest copyright year, in that order of preference.

Pocket Parts (Rule 12.3.1(e))
If you located your statute in a pocket part or soft-cover supplement to the main volume, indicate such in the parenthetical as follows:

> 15 U.S.C.A. § 1051 (West Supp. 2006)
> 11 U.S.C.S. § 301 (LexisNexis 1996 & Supp. 2006). (Note: Parenthetical indicates that the statute is located both in the hardback main volume as well as in the supplement or pocket part.)

Practice Tip

✓ Practitioners seldom include the parenthetical even though it is required by *The Bluebook*. Nearly all practitioners merely end their statutory citations after giving the section number of the statute, as in 35 U.S.C. § 601. Information in the parenthetical about the publisher of an unofficial set is particularly confusing due to merging of many legal publishing companies. *The Bluebook's* Table T.1 refers to some publishers who no longer publish the sets indicated. To determine the publisher whose name should be inserted in a parenthetical, check the copyright page of the set of statutes you use.

Spacing (Rule 6.2(c))
Follow the spacing rules given in Chapter 3 and place adjacent single capitals next to each other with no spaces between them. Always place a space after a section symbol (§) just as you would hit the space bar if you were typing the word "section."

Multiple Sections (Rule 3.4(b))
If you wish to direct the reader to several consecutive sections, give inclusive section numbers (separated by a hyphen) and use two section symbols with no spaces between them. If using a hyphen or dash would be ambiguous, use the word "to." Do not drop digits, because statutes can be numbered so oddly that on encountering the reference "42 U.S.C. §§ 101-04," a reader might think he

or she was being directed to a statute called "section 101, subdivision 4," rather than being directed to read sections 101 through 104. Thus, the correct form is "42 U.S.C. §§ 101-104 (2000)" or "Ga. Code Ann. §§ 14-2-101 to 14-2-114 (1997). "Similarly, do not use the expression "et seq." (meaning "and following") to direct a reader to several sections because it is too imprecise.

Section Symbol (Rule 6.2(c))
In "stand alone" citations, use the section symbol § rather than the word "section" except for the first word of a sentence, which can never be a symbol. Thus, state "Section 107 provides a complete defense" rather than "§ 107 provides a complete defense." In textual sentences, spell out the word "section" except when referring to a provision in the United States Code.

Odds and Ends
- The plural of § is §§.
- Cite to the official code whenever possible (Rule 12.2.1(a)).
- In citations to the Internal Revenue Code, the reference to the title ("26 U.S.C.") may be replaced with "I.R.C." Thus, "26 U.S.C. § 101 (2000)" may be replaced with "I.R.C. § 101 (2000)" (Rule 12.8.1).
- If a statute is known by a popular name, that name may be used with the citation if it would be helpful. For example, "Lanham Act § 44(e), 15 U.S.C. § 1126(e) (2000)" is correct (Rule 12.3.1).
- *The Bluebook* gives little guidance regarding the spacing for parenthetical portions of statutes but generally shows no spacing. Thus, cite "17 U.S.C. § 106(a)" rather than "17 U.S.C. § 106 (a)."

See the Appendix, Examples of State Cases and Statutes, for sample citations for all states and the District of Columbia.

Legislative Materials
(Rule 13; B6.1.6)

On occasion, legal writers discuss the history of certain statutes. For example, they may wish to compare the various versions of a bill, provide background about the intent of the statute according to its sponsor, or quote from floor debates. The material considered during the legislative process is called *legislative history* and may consist of versions of the bill, transcripts of committee hearings held to discuss the bill, committee reports issued after the hearings were held, or floor debates. Although there are other documents making up legislative history (joint resolutions, committee prints, and so forth), only the most commonly cited materials are discussed here.

Following are forms for federal legislative documents. Consult *The Bluebook* for information on citing state legislative documents. State legislative history is cited far less frequently than federal legislative history. Legislative history is not binding on a court. Like secondary authorities (discussed in Chapter 5), it is persuasive, not mandatory.

Bills (Rule 13.2)

Bills are introduced in either the House of Representatives or Senate during a congress. Each congress lasts two years and has two sessions, a first and a second. The first session always occurs in odd-numbered years while the second session always occurs in even-numbered years. The 110th Congress began in January 2007. The 111th Congress begins in January 2009.

Cite bills as follows:

- H.R. 604, 105th Cong. § 3 (1998). This citation signals that the bill was the 604th piece of legislation introduced in the House of Representatives during the 105th Congress and that it was introduced in the second session (the year 1998 conveys this information). It directs the reader to section three of the bill.
- S. 90, 109th Cong. § 1 (2005). This citation references the 90th bill introduced in the Senate in the first session of the 109th Congress and directs the reader to section one of the bill.

Once the bill has been signed by the president, it is a law and should be cited as a statute, namely to U.S.C., U.S.C.A., or U.S.C.S.

Committee Hearings (Rule 13.3)

After a bill is introduced, it is sent to a committee, which will then hold hearings regarding the proposed legislation. Various parties may testify in favor of or against the bill. Transcripts of the committee hearings are published, and citations include the following information: entire title as it appears on the cover of the transcript (treat this title as a book title and, thus, either underscore or italicize it), bill number, subcommittee or committee name (using abbreviations in Table T.9), particular Congress, page of the transcript you wish the reader to review, and year of publication. If you wish, you may identify the witness who testified by using a parenthetical.

Cite committee hearings as follows:

Regulation of the Internet: Hearing on H.R. 114
Before the S. Comm. on Commerce,
106th Cong. 19 (1999) (statement of Stanley Smith,
President, NTI Networks, Inc.).

Committee Reports (Rule 13.4)

After hearings are held, the committee issues a report giving its recommendations regarding the legislation. Citations to committee reports identify which house issued the report, number of the Congress connected by a hyphen to the number of the report, part or page to which the reader is directed, and year of publication.

Cite committee reports as follows:

- H.R. Rep. No. 105-42, at 16 (1998).
- S. Rep. No. 109-442, pt. 3, at 36 (2005).

Floor Debates (Rule 13.5)

A more or less verbatim transcript of debates occurring on the floor of the House of Representatives and Senate is published in the *Congressional Record*, published each day Congress is in session. Initial pamphlets, called daily editions, are eventually replaced by hardbound permanent volumes. When citing to a daily edition, give the full date (using abbreviations shown in Table T.12). Cite to volume, set, page, and date. If desired, you may identify the speaker.

Cite floor debates as follows:

- 135 Cong. Rec. 1911 (1985) (statement of Sen. Thurmond).
- 142 Cong. Rec. H401 (daily ed. Oct. 15, 1990) (statement of Rep. Wolfe). (Note: The "H" preceding "401" indicates that the statements can be found in the House section of the daily edition.)

▪ Uniform Acts (Rule 12.8.4; B6.1.3)

Uniform acts are drafted with the intent they will be adopted by all states. There are approximately 200 uniform acts, the best known of which is the Uniform Commercial Code. Some states adopt the uniform act as drafted, while others make some changes to the act. A reference to a uniform law adopted by a state is cited just as any other statute from that state. West publishes a set entitled *Uniform Laws Annotated*, Master Edition, which publishes more than 160 uniform acts together with related information.

Examples

Uniform act:	U.C.C. § 2-316 (1977).
State version of act:	Cal. Com. Code § 2-316 (West 1998).
Uniform Laws Annotated,	
Master Edition:	Unif. P'ship Act § 29, 14 U.L.A. 164 (1998).

■ **Court Rules** (Rule 12.8.3; B6.1.3)

Cite court rules of evidence or procedure as follows:

Examples

Fed. R. Civ. P. 12(b)(3).
Fed. R. Crim. P. 40.
Fed. R. Evid. 210.
Sup. Ct. R. 33.
Cal. R. Ct. 1.44.

■ **Constitutions** (Rule 11; B7)

U.S. Constitution

Cite the United States Constitution as follows:

Examples

U.S. Const. amend. XIV.
U.S. Const. art. I, § 8.

Remember to convert the large and small typeface you see in *The Bluebook* abbreviation of the word Constitution (CONST.) to ordinary roman type ("Const."). View the inside front and back covers of *The Bluebook* and compare the different presentation styles for law review footnotes and court documents.

State Constitutions

Cite to state constitutions by using the appropriate abbreviations for the states provided in Table T.10 and setting up the citation in a manner similar to that used for the United States Constitution.

Examples

- Cal. Const. art. XXII.
- cNev. Const. art. II, § 4, cl. 6.

Practice Tip

✓ It may look odd to see a lowercase "a" used for "amend." and "art." when referring to constitutions, but that is the rule. Do not give any date if the constitutional provision is still in force.

Exercise for Chapter 4

Correct the following citations. You may need to supply missing information.

1. Fourth Amendment to the U.S. Constitution.

_____

2. Article 3, Section 2, clause 1 of the U.S. Constitution.

_____

3.   Article VI of the California Constitution.

_____

4.   House of Representatives bill number 798, 108th Congress.

_____

5.   Statement of Senator Susan Collins, volume 142 of the Congressional Record, at page 169.

_____

6.   The Patent Reform Act of 2005: Hearing on House of Representatives Bill No. 2795 before the House Subcommittee on Courts, the Internet, and Intellectual Property, held during the 109th Congress, Statement of Larry Ellison, Chief Executive Officer of Oracle Corporation.

_____

_____

7.   Title 17, Section 106 of the United States Code.

_____

8.   Section 401 of Title 42 of United States Code Annotated. (Assume the statute is found only in the pocket part.)

_____

9.   11 United States Code Service Sections 507 through 517 (2003).

_____

10. Rhode Island General Law § 13-30-12.

_____

11. Arizona Revised Statute Annotated Section 19-104 (West).

_____

12. New York General Associations Law Sections 8709-8711.

_____

13. California Public Utilities Section 989.

_____

14.   Uniform Commercial Code Section 3-216.

_____

15.   Federal Rule of Civil Procedure 12(b)(6)

_____

16.   House of Representatives Report Number 108-04, page 62.

_____

5 Secondary Sources

■ Introduction

Sources other than cases, constitutions, statutes, treaties, and administrative regulations are called *secondary sources* and include books, articles, and encyclopedias. Legal writers prefer to cite to primary sources rather than secondary sources because primary sources are mandatory (meaning courts must follow relevant primary sources), while secondary sources are persuasive at best. Note that the examples given in *The Bluebook* for many of the secondary authorities show large and small capitals. As always, practitioners should convert this form to ordinary roman style.

■ Books and Treatises (Rule 15; B8)

Cite books, pamphlets, and other nonperiodical materials by including the following:

- Volume number (if it is a multivolume work).
- Author's name, set forth as the author himself or herself does, including any designation such as "Jr." or "IV." If there are two authors, list them both in the order given in the publication using an ampersand, as in "Leigh Peters & Sofia Bianco." If there are more than two authors, either use the first author's name followed by the signal

"et al." (meaning "and others") or list all of them. Follow the author's name with a comma.

- Title of book (underscored or italicized, depending on preference) given as it appears on the title page. Note that some titles include the author's name, as in *McCarthy on Trademarks and Unfair Competition*. Do not put any punctuation after a book title.
- Page, section, or paragraph, dropping repetitious digits for pages (Rule 3.2(a)), but not for sections or paragraphs (Rule 3.3(b) and (c)).
- Parenthetical information (including any editor or translator, edition of the book if there is more than one edition, and year of publication).

Examples

- 2 J. Thomas McCarthy, *McCarthy on Trademarks and Unfair Competition* § 4-13 (4th ed. 1998).
- 7 Samuel Williston, *Treatise on the Law of Contracts* § 901 (Walter H. Jaeger ed., 3d ed. 1964).
- Sandra Dolan, *Antitrust Law* § 4.06 (Anna Nelson trans., 4th ed. 1997).
- John Harris et al., *Indemnity Protection* ¶¶ 101-106 (1997).

■ **Periodical Materials** (Rule 16; B9)

The publications that law schools periodically produce are generally called *law reviews*. Other periodical publications, such as the *Banking Law Journal*, are published to keep practitioners current in their chosen fields. Law reviews and law journals are frequently cited in court documents because they offer scholarly examinations of various legal topics.

A citation to a periodical generally includes the following:

- Author's full name as used by the author (follow the rules noted previously regarding multiple authors). If a note or comment (typically, a shorter piece) is written by a student, indicate such. (See example below.) Follow the author's name with a comma.
- Title of article written (underscored or italicized) and followed by a comma.

- Reference to the name of the periodical in which the article is published (cite to volume, set, and page, following the spacing and abbreviations shown in Table T.13).
- Year (given in parentheses).

Examples

David J. Hayes, Jr., *Due Process*, 41 Emory L.J. 164 (1995).
Janet R. Sanders, Note, *Juvenile Justice*, 77 Mass. L. Rev. 180 (1995).
Franklin Nelson & Taylor Luce, *The Common Law*, 13 J. Legal Educ. 245 (1990).

■ **Dictionaries** (Rule 15.8; B8)

There are several law dictionaries. They are cited according to the rules governing books and treatises. Give the name of the book, page on which the definition appears, and parenthetical with the edition (if other than the first edition) and year of publication.

Examples

Black's Law Dictionary 905 (8th ed. 2004).
Ballentine's Law Dictionary 54 (3d ed. 1969).

■ **Encyclopedias** (Rule 15.8; B8)

Encyclopedias provide an easy-to-read overview of hundreds of legal topics. There are two national sets (*Corpus Juris Secundum* and *American Jurisprudence, Second Series*) and about ten state-specific sets. Although the explanations of the law are articulate and easy to understand, because their approach is so elementary, encyclopedias are seldom cited in authoritative legal writing. Their citation form includes the following elements:

- Volume number
- Reference to name of set
- Topic name (underscored or italicized)

- Section number
- Year (in parentheses)

Examples

76 Am. Jur. 2d *Trademarks* § 63 (1994).
95 C.J.S. *Venue* § 4 (Supp. 1998). (Note: Parenthetical indicates that the information is found in the pocket part.)
14 Cal. Jur. 3d *Contracts* §§ 14-16 (1994).

■ Restatements (Rule 12.8.5; B6.1.3)

The Restatements, the product of the American Law Institute, aim to restate the law of a particular topic in a clear and concise fashion. Comments and notes on the use of the Restatements follow each articulation of any legal principle. The Restatements are likely the most highly regarded of the secondary authorities and are frequently cited.

Cite to the name of the Restatement, section number, reference to comment (if applicable), and year of publication.

Examples

Restatement (Second) of Torts § 13 (1986).
Restatement (Second) of Contracts § 84 cmt. a (1986).

■ A.L.R. Annotations (Rule 16.6.6)

Scholarly essays or annotations are published in *American Law Reports* on a variety of legal topics and are sufficiently respected that they may be cited in court documents and legal memoranda.

Citations include the following elements:

- Author's full name, followed by a comma
- The word "Annotation" followed by a comma

- Title of the work (underscored or italicized) and followed by a comma
- Reference to volume, set, and page
- Year (in parentheses)

Examples

James W. Gray, Annotation, *Nuisance Theory*, 56 A.L.R.4th 145 (1990).
Lindsey Goodman, Annotation, *Defenses in Discrimination Cases*, 64 A.L.R. Fed. 909 (1996).

Practice Tip

✓ Never cite to a digest. Digests such as West's *Federal Practice Digest* or the *American Digest System* published by West are used as case finders. They help one find the law. They are neither primary nor secondary law themselves and, thus, can never be cited.

Exercise for Chapter 5

Correct the following citations. You may need to supply missing information.

1. The definition of "guardian" appearing on page 440 of Black's Law Dictionary, Eighth Edition, 2004.

2. Volume 7 of the second edition of a book written by Taylor R. Young, Jr., entitled "Health Care Law," sections 27 through 30.

3. A law review article appearing at page 919 of volume 43 of the Boston College Law Review, entitled "Gender and Social Policy" and written by Laura M. Hays.

    _____

4. A discussion of Section 38 of the topic Venue in American Jurisprudence, Second Series, Volume 99.

    _____

5. A 2004 book written by Stephen Bourne and Samuel Tarrant entitled "Securities Regulation," Section 409.

    _____

6. A law review article published in volume 31 (page 909) of the Northern Kentucky Law Review in 2004, entitled "Mandatory Sentencing Guidelines," and written by Stephanie Wilkie-Harris.

    _____

7. An annotation entitled "Judicial Restraint" appearing in A.L.R. Fifth Series in 2004 and written by James J. Butler, IV.

    _____

8. Restatement of Torts, Second Series, Section 39.

    _____

9. Section 19, comment b of the Restatement of Trusts, Second Series.

    _____

10. A November 2004 article written in the Tax Lawyer at page 49 by Cynthia Ann Gonzalez, entitled "Tax Reform: The New Code."

    _____

6 Administrative and Executive Materials, Electronic Databases, The Internet, Record Materials and Court Documents, and Public Domain Citations

▧ Administrative and Executive Materials (Rule 14)

In general, administrative materials consist of the rules, regulations, and other materials of federal administrative agencies (such as the SEC or FCC), adjudications, and various executive materials, such as presidential proclamations and executive orders.

Agency Law

Federal agencies have the power to make rules and regulations, which, if properly promulgated, have the effect of statutes. Moreover, the agencies have the power to issue decisions to enforce their rules. The rules and regulations first appear in a daily pamphlet called the *Federal Register*. The regulations are then codified or organized into 50 titles (highly similar to the arrangement of the *United States Code*) and produced in a set published yearly called the *Code of Federal Regulations*. If the agencies are called on to adjudicate a controversy, the decision may be published in various case reports.

Rules and Regulations (Rule 14.2)

Cite rules and regulations to the *Code of Federal Regulations* (C.F.R.) whenever possible, giving the title number, set name, section or part, and year. Giving the year is critical because a new set of C.F.R. is published each year. If the regulation has a commonly known name, give it before the citation.

Examples

- 18 C.F.R. § 701.254 (2005).
- Cheese Import Regulations, 42 C.F.R. § 131 (2006).

Cite to the *Federal Register* only when the regulation has not yet been published in C.F.R., in which case give also any commonly used name of the regulation. Further, if the *Federal Register* indicates where the regulation will appear in C.F.R., give that information parenthetically. Citations to the *Federal Register* include the volume number, set, page number, and exact date.

Examples

- Standard Industrial Codes, 64 Fed. Reg. 278 (Dec. 6, 2007).
- Federal Contract Regulations for Small Businesses, 60 Fed. Reg. 1801 (Mar. 9, 2007) (to be codified at 22 C.F.R. pt. 120).

Treasury Regulations (Rule 14.5.1)

Treasury regulations are not cited to C.F.R. Use the following form: Treas. Reg. § 42.26(b) (1989).

Administrative Decisions (Rule 14.3)

Official Reporters
Decisions issued by various agencies may be published in the official reporters of the agency. Cite to the official reporter if the decision is found therein. Those reporters (and their correct abbreviations) are listed in Table T.1 of *The Bluebook* (before the instructions given for each state). Cite to (and underscore or italicize) the full reported name of the first-listed private party (namely a party that is not an agency of the government) or the official subject-matter title, volume number, set name, page or paragraph, and year of decision (given in parentheses).

Examples

- *Network Solutions, Inc.*, 18 F.C.C.2d 909 (1998).
- *Stevens Textiles Co.*, 403 N.L.R.B. 120, 124 (1995).

Looseleaf Services (Rule 19)
Not every agency publishes its cases officially. A variety of private publishers (notably Commerce Clearing House, Clark Boardman Callaghan, and Bureau of National Affairs) publish cases and other administrative materials unofficially in sets of binders called "looseleaf services." For example, the *Business Franchise Guide* includes cases, statutes, administrative regulations, and a host of other information relating to franchise law. "Looseleaf" refers to the fact that as new material is released, old pages are taken out of the binders and the new pages are inserted. In some instances, the looseleaf binders are later replaced by bound volumes. Generally, cite decisions in looseleaf services as follows: case name (underscored or italicized), volume, abbreviated title of set, publisher (in parentheses), reference to paragraph or section, court information and date (in parentheses, giving exact date for material found in a looseleaf service and the year only for material found in a bound volume). Older materials or materials awaiting binding may be kept

in semipermanent "transfer binders." Table T.15 in *The Bluebook* provides a list of the most frequently cited looseleaf services, giving their proper abbreviations. If a set is not listed in Table T.15, use Table T.13 to locate appropriate abbreviations so you can construct a title.

Examples

In re Walmart Stores, Inc., 5 Bus. Franchise Guide (CCH) ¶ 42,201 (D.N.J. Aug. 12, 1995).
Davidson Co. v. Emory Inst., 24 Commc'ns Reg. (P & F) ¶ 9019 (S.D.N.Y. May 1, 1997).
In re Sav-All Drug Co., 6 Bankr. L. Rep. (CCH) ¶ 66,180 (Bankr. D. Or. 1995).
In re Jacobs, [1994-1995 Transfer Binder] Fed. Sec. L. Rep. (CCH) ¶ 12,021 (M.D. Pa. 1995).

SEC and Patent Materials (Rules 14.6 and 14.9)

The new Eighteenth Edition of *The Bluebook* has expanded its section on SEC and stock exchange materials and on patents. *The Bluebook* now provides many useful examples for the following SEC materials: no-action letters, SEC releases, stock exchange and NASDAQ rules and manuals, and various filings made with the SEC (including annual reports and proxy statements). (See Rule 14.6.)

Similarly, recognizing the ever-increasing importance of intellectual property law, *The Bluebook* provides several examples for citing both filed and issued patents and specific portions of patents, such as specific fields, figures, and columns. (See Rule 14.9.) An abbreviation for the *Official Gazette of the United States Patent and Trademark Office* is given in Table T.1, for the Board of Patent Appeals and Interferences and for the Trademark Trial and Appeal Board in Table T.7, and for the *United States Patent Quarterly* in Table T.15.

Practice Tip

✓ Although *The Bluebook* provides many forms and examples for administrative materials and services, practitioners often develop their own forms, typically using citation forms suggested or used by various agencies or tribunals. If *Bluebook* rules are ignored for these materials, just ensure consistency in your office. Prepare your own mini citation manual and circulate it to your colleagues so everyone cites uniformly.

Presidential and Executive Materials (Rule 14.7)

Presidents can issue proclamations (for action having no legal effect, such as declaring June 10, 1997 "Girl Scout Appreciation Day") or executive orders (which have the effect of law until a court rules otherwise). Most presidential material is published in title 3 of C.F.R. If the material is also published in U.S.C. (or U.S.C.A. or U.S.C.S), give that citation also. If the presidential material is so recent it is not yet in C.F.R., cite to the *Federal Register* and give the exact date.

Examples

Proclamation No. 7869, 3 C.F.R. 180 (2005).
Proclamation No. 7991, 50 Fed. Reg. 35,012 (Jan. 8, 1998).
Exec. Order No. 13,417, 71 Fed. Reg. 71,459 (Dec. 8, 2006).
Exec. Order No. 13,393, 3 C.F.R. 690 (2004), *reprinted in* 3 U.S.C. § 343 (2005).

■ Lexis and Westlaw (Rule 18.1)

There are two major computerized legal research systems: LexisNexis ("Lexis") (owned by Reed Elsevier Inc.) and Westlaw (owned by Thomson/ West). Although there are some differences between the two systems, they are nearly equal in most respects. Many researchers enjoy using these computerized systems because they are easy to access and provide quick results. Of course, proficiency takes time and practice. The question then becomes, how does one cite to material located via Lexis or Westlaw?

The Eighteenth Edition of *The Bluebook* continues a prejudice against citing to the commercial electronic databases, primarily due to the variance in their availability and permanence. *The Bluebook* (Rule 18) requires the use and citation of traditional printed sources. Only when the material is not available in a printed source or when the traditional source is so obscure that it is practically unavailable should citation be made solely to an electronic source. Nevertheless, *The Bluebook* acknowledges the reliability and authoritativeness of Lexis and Westlaw and prefers these electronic sources to the Internet. (See Rule 18.1.) Thus, cite to an electronic database such as Lexis or Westlaw only when the information is not available in a printed source or when a copy of the source cannot be located because it is so obscure. If a case is reported in conventional print materials, citation to Lexis or Westlaw would be inappropriate.

Similarly, for statutes, Rule 12.2.1 states that one should cite statutes to the official code. If that is unavailable, one may cite to an unofficial code, official session laws, privately published session laws, widely used computer database, looseleaf service, an Internet source, or newspaper, *in that order of preference*. Thus, citing statutes to Lexis or Westlaw can be done only when a federal statute is unavailable in U.S.C., U.S.C.A., U.S.C.S., or any session laws.

Why is citation to electronic databases frowned on when the databases have been in existence for years? Some experts speculate that citing to electronic databases makes retrieval difficult for some judges who may be unskilled in the use of the electronic databases. Over time, this will likely change. For now, however, the general rule is that one should cite to Lexis or Westlaw only when the authority is not available in conventional print form or when the traditional source is so obscure that it is practically unavailable.

For cases, cite as follows: case name, docket number of case, database identifier, and court name and exact date parenthetically. If screen or page numbers have been assigned, indicate such with an asterisk before the relevant number. (See Rule 18.1.1.)

Examples

Cases	*Bowen Assoc. v. Capital Fin. Group,* No. 04-1765, 2006 U.S. App. LEXIS 1202, at *2 (4th Cir. Oct. 8, 2006).
	Green v. Taylor, No. 05-CAS-120, 2007 WL 44102, at *1 (D.N.J. Feb. 10, 2007).
Short Forms	*Bowen,* 2006 U.S. App. LEXIS 1202, at *3.
	Green, 2007 WL 44102, at *2.

For statutes, cite to title, set, and section and then give parenthetically the name of the database and information relating to the currency of the database (rather than giving the year of the code). If the code is published unofficially, give the name of the publisher in the parentheses as well. (See Rule 18.1.2.)

Examples

Statutes

42 U.S.C. § 1204 (LEXIS through 2005 Sess.).

Cal. Educ. Code § 155 (West, Westlaw through 2005 Sess.).

S.D. Codified Laws § 21-103-19 (LEXIS through 2004 Reg. Sess.).

■ **The Internet** (Rule 18.2)

The Eighteenth Edition continues *The Bluebook*'s preference for conventional print materials over electronic sources, primarily because the conventional print sources are more cite worthy. Rule 18.2 provides that traditional printed sources should be used and cited except when the information is unavailable in a printed source or the source is available in a traditional print format, but the content of the Internet source is identical to that of the print version, and a parallel citation to the Internet will significantly improve access to the source. Introduce the parallel Internet source with the phrase *available at*.

Thus, although there are thousands of cases and statutes available for viewing on the Internet, generally you cannot cite to them on the Internet because they are available in conventional print form. In fact, *The Bluebook* states that cases and statutes must be cited first to a traditional source or an electronic database (such as Lexis or Westlaw) except that an Internet source may be cited when the information is not available in a traditional source or electronic database. Nevertheless, if local rules permit or require citation to the Internet, those rules supersede *The Bluebook*.

There are two basic rules for citing to the Internet:

- ● **Internet source as parallel citation.** You may include a parallel citation to an Internet source whose content is identical to a traditional print source if the Internet citation will substantially improve access to the source cited. Give the traditional print source first, follow it with a comma, and introduce the Internet URL information with the phrase *available at.*

Example

Dan L. Burk, *Biotechnology in the Federal Circuits: A Clockwork Lemon,* 46 Ariz. L. Rev. 441 (2004), *available at* http://www.law.arizona.edu/Journals/ALR/ALR2004/vol463.htm.

---

* **Internet source as direct citation.** Many articles and materials exist only on the Internet; there is no print counterpart for them. In such cases, format the citation by analogy to other *Bluebook* rules. For example, if the source is an online journal, cite as you would other journals and periodicals (namely, by using *Bluebook* Rule 16, as in the following example).

Example

Peter Roberts & Canice Chan, *China: The Emergence of a Major New LNG Demand Market in Asia,* (2005), http://www.jonesday.com/pubs/pubs_detail.aspx?pubid=495678403.

If material is undated, indicate the date that the website was last visited, as follows: U.S. Copyright Office Home Page, http://www.copyright.gov (last visited Mar. 15, 2007).

Examples

Case published in print source but available on the Internet:
Feist Publ'ns Inc. v. Rural Tel. Serv. Co., 499 U.S. 340 (1991), *available at* http://caselaw.findlaw.com/scripts/getcase.pl?court=us&vol=499&invol.=340.

Statute published in print source but available on the Internet:
17 U.S.C. § 101 (2000), *available at* http://www4.law.cornell.edu/uscode/17/101.html.

Article available only on the Internet: Brenda Sandburg, *PTO's Destination: Silicon Valley*, (1999), - http://www.lawnewsnet.com/stories.

Practice Tip

✓ *The Bluebook* now gives some guidance on working with unwieldy URLs: If the URL is fairly straightforward, it should be cited as it appears in the address bar. If the URL is overly long or includes several nontextual characters (such as question marks and percentage signs), *The Bluebook* suggests that the root URL be provided and then an explanation of how to access the information should be provided parenthetically.

Example: http://www.megalaw.com (select "State Laws"; then select "California"; then select "Search California Regulations"; then follow hyperlink).

■ Record Materials and Court Documents (Rule 10.8.3; B10; BT.1)

In many instances, legal writers wish to refer in a brief to other pleadings, motions, or materials that make up part of the court's record in a case. For example, a plaintiff may wish to draw the court's attention to an allegation made by the defendant in an answer to a complaint. *The Bluebook* offers only minimal guidance.

Follow these citation tips:

- Enclose the reference in parentheses, putting a period inside the parentheses if the parenthetical reference stands alone at the end of a sentence and surrounding the parentheses with no punctuation if the reference appears as a clause within a sentence.
- You may string references together using semicolons.
- Use the abbreviations shown in Table BT.1 of *The Bluebook*.
- Omit articles and prepositions from the title of a court document, unless confusion would result.

- You should use "at" when referring to pages in an appellate record. You are usually not required to use "at" before other pinpoint citations. Do not use "at" before a section or paragraph symbol.
- Ensure consistency in your citation form.
- Use the "hereinafter" form to establish an abbreviation of a long title described in text after you have cited the material in full the first time, as follows: "Juvenile Office Probation Sentencing Report" [hereinafter "Sentencing Report"].
  Note: *The Bluebook* states that the word "hereinafter" and the shortened from appear in square brackets rather than in rounded parentheses, but practitioners usually use parentheses.

Example

- Defendant has alleged that he revoked his acceptance of the contract. (Def.'s Answer to Compl. ¶ 3.) Nevertheless, Defendant has acknowledged that the purported revocation was mailed to Plaintiff only after Plaintiff had signed and delivered the contract. (Def.'s Dep. 26:1-4, Jan. 31, 2004.) As discussed in Plaintiff's Motion for Summary Judgment [hereinafter "Motion"] and other witnesses have confirmed (Taylor Aff. ¶ 3), the mailing of the revocation was effected only after execution and delivery of the contract by Plaintiff. (Gregson Decl. ¶ 14; Harrison Aff. ¶ 7; Franklin Admis. ¶ 9.)

▨ Public Domain Citation
(Rule 10.3.3)

Introduction

Ever-increasing numbers of cases and statutes have begun appearing on the Internet. However, the traditional method of citing to volume and page numbers in printed books of case reports cannot be used effectively for new opinions appearing on the Internet because the printed case books are not published for several weeks (or even months) after an opinion is released on the Internet. Therefore, both the American Bar Association (ABA) and the American Association of Law Libraries (AALL) have recommended that courts adopt a uniform citation system that is equally adaptable whether authorities are located in conventional printed materials or through electronic means. The Department of Justice has recommended that the federal courts adopt the ABA proposal to ensure consistency among the federal courts.

The proposed system is variously called "public domain," "vendor neutral," or "medium neutral" because the citation will look the same whether the source is found in print or electronic media. West, however, has called public domain citations "nowhere cite[s]," believing the citations do not refer readers to any actual, physical location for a case.

ABA Approach

Since 1996, the ABA has formally recommended to federal and state courts that they adopt a universal and medium neutral citation system. The ABA approach was largely patterned after the AALL solution. The ABA recommended that courts assign the citation at the time decisions are released to the public to enable readers to easily locate material whether they review the case in print form or on the Internet. Citations would include the following:

- Case name
- Year of decision
- The state's two-character postal code
- Identification of court issuing the opinion (unless it is the highest court)
- Sequential number of the decision
- Reference to specific numbered paragraphs in which material is located

The ABA also recommended that citations include parallel citations until electronic publications become commonly used by practitioners and judges. The parallel citation would not include any pinpoint citations (that is, a reference to the specific page on which material appears).

Example   *(for federal case)*

Allen v. Rousch, 1998 4 Cir. 24, 14, 35 F.3d 107.

The citation in this example tells the reader that the case name is *Allen v. Rousch,* that it was the 24th case decided in 1998 by the Fourth Circuit Court of Appeals, and that the reader is directed to paragraph 14 within the case. The parallel citation then tells the reader the case is located in volume 35 of the *Federal Reporter,* Third Series, beginning at page 107. *The Bluebook* (Table T.1) provides the following format for Sixth Circuit cases: *Shea v. Wilson,* 1998 FED App. 218P (6th Cir.).

The Bluebook Approach (Rule 10.3.3)

Bluebook Rule 10.3.3 states that if it is available, a parallel citation to the appropriate regional reporter *must* be provided in addition to a public domain citation. Thus, the public domain citation really only replaces the official citation. The citation should include the case name, year of decision, the state's two-character postal code (given in Table T.1), the court abbreviation (given in Table T.7) unless the court is the state's highest court, sequential number of the decision, an uppercase "U" if the decision is unpublished, and a paragraph number when referring to specific material in the case.

Example

Wade v. Lee, 2003 ND 138, ¶ 7, 670 N.W.2d 18, 22.

Which states have adopted official public domain citation formats such that you would use the format described herein rather than the usual approach consisting of case name, official citation, regional citation, and year of decision? At the time of publication of the Sixteenth Edition of *The Bluebook* in 1996, only Louisiana had adopted a public domain citation format. Since that time, Maine, Mississippi, Montana, New Mexico, North Dakota, Ohio, Oklahoma, Pennsylvania (for Superior Court cases only), South Dakota, Utah, Vermont, Wisconsin, and Wyoming have adopted public domain citation systems, and other states are considering such adoption. If you cite cases from these states, check state and local court rules regarding citation form. In the absence of any information, follow the format shown in *The Bluebook.* Table T.1 provides an example for each of the above-listed states. Additional information can be located at the website for the ABA Legal Technology Resource Center at http://www.abanet.org/tech/ltrc/research/citation/home.html.

There is much variation from state to state in spacing and abbreviations in these public domain citations. Some states neither underscore nor italicize case names in public domain citations. Additional information may be available at your state's home page. Access the website for MegaLaw (http://megalaw.com) and then select "State Law" and review your state's court rules. Information about citation form and other state-specific rules may be provided at the site. Additionally, Table T.1 provides references to each state's judicial website.

Note that *The Bluebook* discussion of public domain citations only relates to state court cases. There is no indication in *The Bluebook* that using a public domain citation for any federal case (other than one from the Sixth Circuit) is appropriate. In fact, most federal court judges are adamantly opposed to public domain citations, primarily because the burden of numbering paragraphs and assigning sequential opinion numbers would fall on the courts themselves. Nevertheless, the Sixth Circuit Court of Appeals has made the use of a public domain citation optional in the Sixth Circuit and an example is shown in Table T.1., in Chapter Three of this text, and above.

Exercise for Chapter 6

Correct each citation. You may need to supply or create missing information. Assume citations are "stand-alone" citations.

1. Defendant's deposition, taken on April 14, 2005, at page 109.

   _____

2. Plaintiff's response to defendant's interrogatory number 32.

   _____

3. Exhibit F.

   _____

4. Paragraph 14 of Defendant's Counterclaim.

   _____

5.   Plaintiffs' Motion to Dismiss, paragraphs 21-31.

---

6.   *Laughlin v. Kmart Corp.*, volume 3, Blue Sky Law Reports, Paragraph 13, District Court of New Jersey, August 12, 2003).

---

7.   Presidential Proclamation Number 7918. (Assume the material is not available in C.F.R.)

---

8.   Executive Order 13,350. (Assume the material is available in C.F.R.)

---

9.   Section 203.211 of title 24 of the Code of Federal Regulations.

---

10. Hardy v. Shook, No. 04-123 (Third Circuit, May 28, 2005), Westlaw 13499.

---

11. An article entitled "The Madrid Protocol," written by Neil Jones in 2004 and located only at www.uspto.gov/web/trademarks/madrid/madridindex.htm.

---

12. The case *Harper v. Gregory Association,* 535 U.S. 16 (2005), available at the website of the U.S. Supreme Court.

---

13. "Personnel Management: Employee Surveys," volume 70 of the Federal Register, pages 54,658-54,660, September 16, 2005 (to be codified at 42 C.F.R. part 209).

---

14. Give the public domain citation (with pinpoints) for the nineteenth 2001 South Dakota Supreme Court case *People v. Talbott*.

---

15. Figure 3 of U.S. Patent Number 6102103, filed on February 12, 2005.

7

Punctuation, Quotations, Omissions, Alterations, and Parentheticals

▪ Punctuation for Citations
(Rules 1.1 and 1.4; B2)

There are only three punctuation marks used after a citation is given: periods, commas, and semicolons. Use these marks as follows:

- Use a period to follow a citation when it supports or contradicts a previous declaratory sentence (Rule 1.1; B2).

Example

- Trademarks can be abandoned through nonuse. *Powell Co. v. Hart*, 482 U.S. 15 (1990). (Note: Such a citation ending with a period is a "stand-alone" citation, and thus, any of the more than 160 words in Table T.6 in

The Bluebook would be abbreviated in the case name, including the first word in the case name.)

- Use a comma to follow a citation when the citation supports or contradicts only part of a sentence (Rule 1.1; B2).

Example

- Although trademarks can be abandoned by nonuse, *Powell Co. v. Hart*, 482 U.S. 15 (1990), evidence of nonuse must be clear and convincing, *Gen. Cas. Constr. Co. v. Kaye*, 483 U.S. 190 (1992).

- Use a semicolon to separate citations from each other when more than one citation supports or contradicts a previous statement, namely, when the citations are placed in a "string." (See Rule 1.4.) Note that the string is often preceded by a signal such as *see, but see*, and so forth.

Practice Tip

✓ In a citation string, the most helpful or authoritative citation should be placed first. Thereafter, the citations must be listed in the hierarchical order set forth in Rule 1.4, as follows:

- Statutes (first federal and then state statutes);
- Federal cases (starting with U.S. Supreme Court cases, then courts of appeal cases, and then district court cases, but treat all courts of appeal as one court and all district courts as one court, and within each group list newer cases before older ones); and
- State cases, listed alphabetically by state. (If there are several cases from the same state, list those from higher courts before those from lower courts, and within each grouping, list newer cases before older ones.)

Example

- A general partnership agreement need not be in writing. See *Allen v. James Bus. Co.*, 433 F.2d 18 (8th Cir. 1990); *Daly v. Young*, 420 F.2d 26 (4th Cir. 1985); *Hardy v. Oakland Co.*, 401 N.E.2d 18 (Mass. 1994); *Malone v. Midwestern Realty Org.*, 414 N.E.2d 89 (Mass. App. Ct. 1996); *Powell v. Lyden Co.*, 412 N.E.2d 149 (Mass. App. Ct. 1995).

■ **Quotations** (Rule 5; B5.1.2 and B12)

Introduction — Pinpoint Cites (Rule 3.2)

When quoting from an authority you must give the specific page on or section at which the quotation appears. What if you are merely paraphrasing the authority rather than directly quoting from it? *The Bluebook* states that these pinpoint cites are critical for any cited proposition because they "provide the only means by which you can direct the reader to the exact page that contains the information or quotation on which you are relying for support." (B5.1.2.) Thus, give pinpoints for direct quotations and for paraphrased material.

Example

Copyrights are governed by federal law. *Wade v. Grayson*, 409 U.S. 14, 16 (1988); *Donoghue v. Cook*, 201 S.E.2d 409, 414 (Va. 1995).

The second page number is called a "pinpoint citation" because you are pinpointing for the reader exactly where to find material you are discussing. Occasionally, the second number is called a "jump citation," indicating you are asking the reader to jump to a certain page within a source.

The general practice is to always include the pinpoint citation, even if you are not directly quoting from a source. Why? It is the courteous approach, saving the reader from endlessly hunting through the authority trying to find the material you discuss. Moreover, if your research says what you claim it does, you should have no concern about allowing someone to verify your statements through the use of pinpoint citations. If a case has parallel citations, give the pinpoint citation for each.

Shorter Quotations (Rule 5.1(b))

If your quotation is 49 words or fewer, do not indent it. Merely keep the quotation in the regular portion of your narrative. Use quotation marks (" ") to designate which material is being quoted, and *always* place commas and periods inside the quotation marks, even if your quote is only one word long. Other punctuation marks should be placed inside your quotation marks only if they are part of the material quoted. Should you count the words in a quote to determine its length? Yes, absolutely; you should always count the words.

Example

Courts have consistently held that while directors and officers of a corporation are not ordinarily liable for corporate obligations, this shield of limited liability will be pierced "when necessary to prevent fraud or injustice." *Carter v. Andrews Equip. Co.*, 482 U.S. 190, 194-95 (1995).

Lengthy Quotations (Rule 5.1(a); B12)

A quotation that is 50 words or longer should be indented 10 spaces left and right and single-spaced. Because the writing will appear as a chunk of words on the paper, this type of quotation is often referred to as a "block quotation." Do not use quotation marks for a block quotation. The fact that material is indented or blocked signals to the reader that it is a quotation.

Authors often place the citation for the quoted material within the indented block itself. This is incorrect. Only quoted material belongs in the block. The citation should be placed at the left margin on the first new line immediately following the block quotation (which appears two lines below the block quotation). If you then start a new paragraph, the citation may appear to be floating or hanging in space. Although odd-looking, this presentation is correct. Follow this format:

> Xxxxxxxxxxxxxxxxxxxxxxxxxxxxxxxxxxxxxxxxxxxxxxxxxxxxxxxxxxxxxxxxxx
> xxxxxxxxxxxxxxxxxxxxxxxxxxxxxxxxxxxxxxxxxxxxxxxxxxxxxxxxxxxxxxxxxx
> xxxxxxxxxxxxxxxxxxxxxxxxxxxxxxxxxxxxxxxxxxxxxxxxxxxxxxxxxxxxxxxxxx
> xxxxxxxxxxxx

Lee v. Henry, 505 U.S. 6, 10 (1998).

Practice Tip

✓ You often see legal writers block-indenting quotes that are fewer than 50 words. Generally, this is done for stylistic reasons, so that the material is more dramatically presented to the reader. Many judges, however, are sticklers for *Bluebook* rules, so using a block for a short quotation merely for drama purposes may be disfavored.

Odds and Ends

- **Showing emphasis.** Do not use the expression "emphasis in original" if a word is italicized or otherwise emphasized in the original quotation. In legal writing, it is presumed that readers are sophisticated, and they will thus assume you have reproduced a quotation scrupulously. It is only when you change a quotation, perhaps by italicizing a word for emphasis, that you will indicate "emphasis added" (Rule 5.2). For example, the following is correct: The Court stated, "these limited liability partners are not personally liable for the acts of *misconduct* of their co-partners." *Randall v. Cox,* 500 U.S. 160, 165 (1994) (emphasis added). If you are underscoring rather than italicizing, use a solid unbroken line to show words you have emphasized.

- **Multiple pages.** If a quotation spans more than one page, give the inclusive page numbers, separated by a hyphen or dash, retaining the last two digits, but striking other repetitious digits, as follows: *Nelson v. Nelson,* 601 P.2d 920, 922-26 (Nev. 1995). (Rule 3.2(a)).

- **Quotation on first page.** If the material you discuss or quote appears on the first page of a source, repeat the page, as follows: Guy Talbot, *Bankruptcy Preferences,* 37 How. L.J. 18, 18 (1990). (Rule 3.2(a)).

- **Quotations within quotations.** In narrative text, if your quotation itself quotes from another source, switch from double quotation marks to single quotation marks to double quotation marks, and so forth (Rule 5.1(b)). In a block quotation, quotation marks should appear as they do in the original source (Rule 5.1(a)).

- **Nonconsecutive pages.** If referring to nonconsecutive pages, set the citation up as follows: *Amey v. Scalise,* 502 U.S. 14, 18, 22 (1997). (Rule 3.2(a)).

- **Repeated references.** If a point is repeatedly made throughout a source, omit the pinpoint citation and use the word "*passim*," which means "everywhere," as follows: *Marks v. Carson*, 506 U.S. 180 *passim* (1998). Note that there is no comma between the page number and *passim* (Rule 3.2(a)).

- **Paragraph structure.** If a quotation you are indenting is a new paragraph in the original source, indicate such by also indenting the first line of your block quotation. If your block quotation includes several paragraphs from the original material, a blank line should separate each paragraph from the next, and each paragraph within the block should be indented to mimic the paragraph structure of the original quote. Show the omission of an entire paragraph by four indented periods on a separate line (Rule 5.1(a)).

- **Line breaks.** *The Blubook* gives no guidence on breaking a citation from one line to the next. Use good judgment, and break the citation in a way that is not confusing or visually distracting to the reader.

Example

> Xxxxxxxxxxxxxxxxxxxxxxxxxxxxxxxxxx xxxxxxxxxxxxxxxxxxxxxxxxxxxxxxxxxxxxx xxxxxxxxxxxxxxxxxxxxxxxxxxxxxxxxxxxxxx.
>
> . . . .
> Xxxxxxxxxxxxxxxxxxxxxxxxxxxxxxxxxx xxxxxxxxxxxxxxxxxxxxxxxxxxxxxxxxxxx xxxxxxxxxxxxxxxxxxxxxxxxxxxxxxxxxxxxx.

- **Piggybacking.** If your quotation is originally from a case other than the one you are relying on, indicate such as follows: "Employers are vicariously liable for 'certain acts of their employees.'" *Edwards v. Lane*, 501 U.S. 294, 299 (1998) (quoting *O'Connor v. Schultz*, 450 U.S. 24, 27 (1990)). (Rules 5.2(e) and 10.6.2).

- **Justification.** *The Bluebook* (B12) states that block quotations are fully justified (meaning that the lines of typing end at the same place along the left- and right-hand margins). Check your firm practice because some attorneys prefer a "ragged" right edge.

■ Omissions (Rule 5.3)

It is acceptable to omit material from a quotation, as long as you indicate such. Use an *ellipsis* (three periods separated from each other by spaces which are preceded and followed by spaces) to show omitted material.

Example

"Punitive damages must be . . . based upon actual damages." *Harvey Ltd. v. Viacor, Inc.*, 451 U.S. 91, 97 (1990).

Follow these additional rules:

- To show that you omitted material at the end of a sentence, use four periods (three for the ellipsis and one to show the period at the end of the sentence), as follows: "A landlord must provide habitable premises to a tenant . . . ." Note that a space is placed before the first period.
- If you quote matter, then omit matter and quote additional material, set up the quotation as follows: "A corporation can be dissolved by the state. . . . [A]n involuntary dissolution involves a court proceeding." Note that there is no space after the word "state" and before the first period. Why? You are telling the reader that you did not omit any part of the first sentence. Thus, you retain its original punctuation.
- If you are merely quoting a phrase within a sentence, you do not need an ellipsis. Set up such a quotation as follows: The Court further held that "sexual harassment is prohibited under Title VII" and is "a significant workplace problem."
- Never use an ellipsis to begin a quotation. Use a bracketed letter to show that language beginning a sentence has been omitted, as follows: "[I]t is axiomatic that damages are awarded for breach of contract." The placement of an uppercase "I" in the brackets shows that in the original quotation the "I" was a lowercase letter. This signals to the reader that the word "it" was not the first word of the sentence.
- It is acceptable to omit citations that appear in the middle of a quotation (generally because they clutter the quotation). Simply give your quotation and at the end include the phrase "citations omitted" in a parenthetical, as follows: "Consent is a defense to the tort of battery." *May v. Jeffers*, 681 P.2d 18, 25 (Cal. 1994) (citations omitted).

■ Alterations (Rule 5.2)

An alteration is a minor change in a quote, such as changing a letter from upper- to lowercase (or vice versa), pluralizing or singularizing a word, changing a tense, correcting spelling, or adding a word. Use square brackets to show alterations.

Example

"[I]nfringement of trademarks can be shown by proof of [actual] confusion."

The use of the brackets in the preceding example tells the reader that in the original quotation the word "infringement" started with a lowercase "i" and that the word "actual" did not appear. Rather, the author inserted the word "actual" for purposes of style or readability.

Example

"The landlord[s] failed to act in accordance with contractual duties."

The use of the brackets in this example tells the reader that in the original quotation the word "landlord" was singular. Here, the author wants to pluralize the word for purposes of style. An empty bracket in a word, for example, "action[ ]," tells the reader that in the original quotation there was another letter in the word (clearly, the word was "actions").

■ Parentheticals (Rule 10.6; B5.1.4; B11)

Legal writers often use parenthetical expressions to convey certain information (other than dates). Generally parentheticals fall into two categories.

- **Weight of authority.** Some parentheticals tell the reader something about the strength or weakness of the citation. Some of the more frequently used parentheticals to show weight of authority are as follows: en banc, 5-4 decision, mem. (for memorandum decisions, namely those in which a court issues a holding but gives either no or very little opinion), per curiam (meaning "by the court," indicating an opinion in which no particular author is identified), and identifications of concurring and dissenting opinions.

Examples

- The Court upheld the doctrine of equivalents. *Carley v. Bennett*, 404 U.S. 16, 19-21 (1985) (9-0 decision).
- The endorsement test should be used in First Amendment cases examining separation of church and state. *Sherman v. Carlson*, 410 U.S. 610, 646 (1987) (O'Connor, J., dissenting).
  Note: Readers will always assume you are relying on the majority opinion. Thus, if you rely on a dissenting or concurring opinion, you must indicate such by the use of a parenthetical.

- **Explanatory parentheticals.** Explanatory parentheticals are those that provide some explanation about the case. They should be given after parentheticals that indicate the weight of authority but before any subsequent history. Note that the expression in the parenthetical usually begins with a present participle (a verb ending in "ing" such as "holding" or "rejecting"). They may also consist of an entire quoted sentence or a short statement. (B11)

Remember that we have already discussed certain parenthetical expressions, namely the expressions "citations omitted," used when you wish to delete citations from the middle of your quotation and "piggybacking," used to indicate that your case relied on or quoted from an earlier case.

Examples

- *Lowell v. Lynn*, 689 F.2d 191, 194-97 (D.C. Cir. 1990) (3-0 decision) (holding that trademarks can be diluted either by blurring or tarnishment).

- *Miller v. Malone Dev. Fed'n,* 13 F. Supp. 2d 101, 104 (C.D. Cal. 1998) (rejecting the doctrine of reverse equivalents), *aff'd,* 40 F.3d 16 (9th Cir. 1999).
- *Raymond v. Timmons,* 489 U.S. 16, 18 (1995) (5-4 decision) (quoting *Jamison v. Woods,* 456 U.S. 890, 895 (1990)).

Practice Tip

✓ Parenthetical information should appear in the following order:

- Weight of authority parentheticals (such as "6-3 decision");
- "Piggybacking" parentheticals (namely, those starting with the words "quoting" or "citing"); and
- Explanatory parentheticals (those that explain something about the case, usually starting with phrases such as a "noting that" or "holding that" or similar "ing" words.)

Exercise for Chapter 7

Correct the following statements and citations. There may be more than one thing wrong with each citation, and you may need to create missing information. Unless otherwise directed, assume that state court cases are being cited in internal office memoranda.

1. In Kramer v. Jarvis, 86 F. Supp.2d 342 (Middle District Pennsylvania 1999), the Court held that "...parties to a contract must be competent to enter into that contract."

_____

_____

2. Indicate that the following 2005 Ninth Circuit case was a per curiam decision that was later affirmed by the U.S. Supreme Court the same year; *Bains LLC v. Arco Products Co.,* 405 F.3d 764.

_____

_____

3. In the following quotation, omit the word "a," pluralize the word "figure," and omit the phrase "for the truth of the statement": "Statements made about a public figure are wrongful if they are made with actual malice, meaning with reckless disregard for the truth of the statement."

_____

_____

4. "Battery is a harmful and offensive touching of another." *Nelson v. Campbell,* 347 F.3d 910 (11th Cir. 2003); *Jacobson v. Farley,* 901 P.2d 45 (Calif. 1990); *Vives v. City of New York,* 405 F.3d 115, 122 (2nd Cir. 2004); *Harris v. Consolidated Transportation Department,* 687 So. 2d 118, 121 (Ala. 1994).

_____

_____

_____

5. "Defamation is publication of false information about another that harms the other's reputation." *Agostini v. Felton,* 521 U.S. 203 (1997) (dissenting opinion by Justice O'Connor) (original quotation appears in the middle of a sentence.

_____

_____

6. Using appropriate parentheticals, indicate that the following is a 9-0 decision that held that general partners have unlimited personal liability. *Crawford v. Washington,* 367 F.3rd 915, 920-922 (D. C. Circuit 2003), reversed at 541 U.S. 36 (2004).

_____

_____

_____

7. Show that you emphasized the phrase "whether it arises in tort or con-
    tract" in the following quotation: "A limited liability company is an entirely
    new form of business enterprise that provides full protection from
    personal liability whether it arises in tort or contract." *Wright v. Benedict
    Construction Co.,* 701 S.E. 2d 410, 414-416 (Georgia 1988).

    _____

    _____

    _____

8. The Court held that "actual malice must be shown for a public figure to
    recover punitive damages in a libel action." *Horn v. Banks,* 536 U.S. 266,
    271 (2002). Make the following changes: Omit the phrase "for a public
    figure," emphasize the word "libel," start your quote with the word "mal-
    ice," and indicate that you omitted a citation from your quote.

    _____

    _____

    _____

8 Short Forms, Signals, Related Authority, and Capitalization

◾ **Short Forms** (Rule 4; Bluepages *passim*)

Citation form is difficult and painstaking. Thus, any time you can avoid giving a citation in full, you should. In general, once a citation is given in full, you may later use a "short form" of it. *The Bluebook* states that short forms may be used if it will be clear to the reader what is being referenced, the earlier full citation is in the same general discussion, and the reader can quickly locate the earlier full citation. Use of the short forms is optional, not mandatory. Do not give a short form until you have given the full citation.

Id. (Rule 4.1)

"*Id.*" is a signal meaning "in the same place" that instructs a reader to return to the immediately preceding citation, no matter what it is. Follow these four rules:

- The word *id.* is itself an abbreviation. Thus, it is always followed by a period.

- *Id.* is a foreign word. Thus, it should be italicized or underscored. (Italicize or underscore the period, as follows: *id.* or <u>id.</u>)
- *Id.* can appear by itself, in which case it starts with a capital letter, or it can appear as a clause in the middle of a sentence, in which case it begins with a lowercase letter.
- The use of *id.* by itself tells the reader to go back to the immediately preceding authority. If you wish to send the reader to a different page, section, or paragraph within that authority, indicate that as shown in the following example.

Example

- The Court flatly announced its support for the doctrine of joint and several liability. *Farley v. Dayton-Hudson, Inc.*, 520 U.S. 16, 19 (1998). Thus, liability may be imposed upon any partner in a general partnership. *Id.* If, however, creditors know a partner has no authority to do a particular act, other partners may be insulated from liability. *Id.* at 26.

Three additional tips on using *id.* are:

- The use of *id.* for a case with a parallel citation does not significantly shorten the citation when you send the reader to a different page. For example, if the first citation is *Kenney v. Plaisance*, 231 Va. 16, 18, 204 S.E.2d 424, 427 (1990), the *id.* form is as follows: *Id.* at 21, 204 S.E.2d at 430. *Id.* only takes the place of the official citation.
- You cannot use *id.* when the preceding citation includes more than one source. For example, if a string citation or footnote contains more than one citation, you cannot use *id.* (otherwise, the reader will not know to which of the preceding references the *"id."* signals refers).
- Note that per Rule 3.3, you cannot use the word "at" before a section sign (§) or a paragraph symbol (¶).

Examples

First reference (case page):   *Wilson v. Preston*, 490 U.S. 14, 16 (1995).
Second reference (case page):   *Id.* at 21.
Third reference (case page):   *Id.* at 24.

First reference (section sign):	Edward Riley, *Patent Practice* § 101 (1995).
Second reference (section sign):	*Id.* § 104. (Note: The word "at" is not used.)

Supra (Rule 4.2; B8.2)

Supra means "above" and is a signal used to send a reader to a preceding citation, but not an immediately preceding citation. Note, however, that *supra* cannot be used to refer to primary authorities such as cases, statutes, regulations, constitutions, or to Restatements, or many legislative materials. It is thus used nearly exclusively to refer to previously cited books, law review and journal articles, and other secondary authorities. It must appear with the name of an author or some other identifying word rather than merely by itself, as does *id.* Although *The Bluebook* is clear that *supra* may not be used as a short form for cases or other primary authorities, some practitioners ignore this rule.

Examples

Page one of brief:	Eve Jones, *Due Process,* 36 N.C. L. Rev. 401, 408 (1995).
Page two of brief:	*Li v. Li,* 482 U.S. 120, 126 (1985).
Page three of brief:	Jones, *supra.* or Jones, *supra,* at 412.

Internal Cross-References (Rule 3.5)

Note that in the preceding example, the use of *supra* directs the reader to the page within Eve Jones's article but does not tell the reader where exactly in your brief the reader will find your original citation to Eve Jones's article. Should you include this information? *The Bluebook* does not require that you tell the reader where in your document he or she will locate the previous citation but states you may do so (Rule 3.5). Use the following form: "Jones, *supra* p. 2, at 414" (directing the reader to page two of your document and then instructing the reader to review page 414 of Eve Jones's article). Note that "p." and "pp." are used only to direct a reader to pages within your document and not to pages within the published authority you are discussing.

When is *supra* followed by a comma? *Supra* is followed by a comma when you are directing the reader to the page or section of the previously cited published authority, as in "Jones, *supra,* at 414." When you are directing the reader to a previous page within your document — such as "Jones, *supra* p. 2, at 414." — there is no comma following the signal.

On some occasions, a brief may use the signal *infra,* meaning "below," to send a reader to a later discussion in the document, as in, "The issue of reckless conduct is discussed in Section IV, *infra.*" The rules governing *supra* apply equally to *infra.* It is also likely that you will encounter *infra* in indexes or texts. Thus, in Chapter 7 of a textbook you may be informed, "For a further discussion of this topic, see Chapter 10, *infra.*"

Use of "Hereinafter" (Rule 4.2(b))

Use "hereinafter" to abbreviate the name of a secondary authority that is long and cumbersome. Enclose the form in brackets. (Note that practitioners tend to use rounded parentheses rather than square brackets.) For example, use the following format: *Sonny Bono Copyright Term Extension Act: Hearings on S. 562 Before the H. Comm. on Energy and Commerce,* 105th Cong. 121 (1997) [hereinafter *Copyright Hearings*]. Note two critical items: First, as with *supra* and *infra,* you cannot use "hereinafter" to refer to primary authorities (meaning you cannot use it as a shorthand signal for a case, statute, regulation, or constitution); and second, once you establish the shorthand abbreviation, you must consistently use it thereafter. Thus, any later reference to the preceding hearings must consistently be called *Copyright Hearings.* This later shortened reference will usually appear with *supra* as in the following: *Copyright Hearings, supra.*

Short Forms for Cases (Rule 10.9(a); B5.2)

What if you cite a case on page two of your brief, then you cite a book on page three, and you wish to cite the case again on page four? You cannot use *id.* because that signal will send the reader to the book that is the immediately preceding citation. You cannot use *supra* because that signal cannot be used to send a reader to a case. Assume the case you cited on page one is *Li v. Li,* 482 U.S. 120, 126 (1985). There are three alternatives you may use.

- Option 1 (B5.2):   *Li,* 482 U.S. at 128.
- Option 2 (B5.2):   482 U.S. at 128.

- Option 3 (Rule 10.9(c)B5.3): Use *"Li,"* with no further citation, if you have cited *Li* in the same general discussion, for example, "In *Li*, the Court also held...."

You may choose the most appropriate option as long as the reader will have no doubt as to which case you are discussing. Thus, use options 2 and 3 only when you have been discussing the authority with such frequency that the reader will have no trouble locating the earlier citation. With regard to option 3, *The Bluebook* does not define the meaning of the term "same general discussion." Some authors view each section of a brief or memorandum as a separate discussion. A reference in a later-numbered section is thus not "in the same general discussion" and requires use of either option 1 or option 2. Use common sense, realizing that if you have not mentioned the *Li* case in several pages, the reader may have difficulty remembering or finding the citation if you only refer to it by name. In such instances, help the reader by giving more rather than less information.

For cases with parallel citations, the short forms are not particularly short. For example, if your first citation was *Young v. Barwich*, 231 Va. 106, 108, 320 S.E.2d 114, 118 (1990), the later citation (assuming you cannot use *id.* because there is an intervening citation) is one of the following:

- *Young*, 231 Va. at 110, 320 S.E.2d at 120.
- 231 Va. at 110, 320 S.E.2d at 120.
- "In *Young*, the court also noted...."

Practice Tip

✓ Although you should generally use the plaintiff's name when sending a reader back to a case, use the defendant's name if the plaintiff's name is a governmental or other common litigant such as "State" or "United States."

Short Forms for Other Authorities

Use the following short forms for authorities other than cases:

- For statutes and regulations, the first citation should be complete. Later references may use any form that clearly identifies the material (B6.2). Thus, the first reference to a statute would be 17 U.S.C.A. § 101

(West 1998), while the later reference could be *id.*, 17 U.S.C.A. § 101, or § 101 (Rule 12.9; B6.2).

- For constitutions, do not use any short form other than *id.* (Rule 11; B7).
- For books, law reviews, and other secondary authorities, use *id.* to send the reader to an immediately preceding authority and *supra* (with author's name or other identifying information) to send a reader to a source that is not immediately preceding, as in "McCarthy, *supra*, § 14.20." (Rule 4.2; B8.2).

Practice Tips

✓ The words or abbreviations *id., supra,* and *infra* are always underscored or italicized, but "hereinafter" is not.

✓ When using short forms for cases, do not include any subsequent history.

✓ Some practitioners follow *Bluebook* rules for law review footnotes for the use of short forms, meaning tha they only use a short form if the full citation can be found in one of the preceding five footnotes (Rule 10.9). This rule relates solely to law review footnotes and is not required for practitioners.

■ Signals (Rule 1.2; B4)

Introduction

Authorities cited by legal writers may support or contradict statements made by the writer or may merely provide background material. Citation signals allow a writer to indicate such without having to explain in full the specific manner in which the cited authority is used. Signals are thus a form of code, instantly conveying information to a reader. Unfortunately, cracking the code is difficult and uncertain due to the vague manner in which *The Bluebook* directs a writer as to the use of the signals.

Signals are divided into several categories: those that show support, those that suggest a useful comparison, those that indicate contradiction, and those that indicate background material. They precede case names or other authorities as follows: *See Brown v. Casey,* 500 U.S. 490, 495-98 (1998). If no signal is used before a citation, the reader should assume that the cited authority directly states the proposition, identifies the source of a quotation, or identifies an authority mentioned in the preceding text. The signal *see* indicates that the cited authority clearly supports the principle stated by the author. *See* is used instead of "no signal" when the proposition is not directly stated by the cited authority but obviously follows from it.

The situation is complicated by the fact that over the years, the use of certain signals has shifted. For example, until the Sixteenth Edition, the signal *contra* informed a reader that the cited authority directly stated the contrary of the proposition. The signal *contra* did not exist in the Sixteenth Edition but reappeared in the Seventeenth Edition. Thus, analyzing briefs, documents, and articles written prior to late 2000 (when the Seventeenth Edition was issued) results in a different interpretation of some signals. (See Figure 8-1 for a chart showing changes in signals.) The Eighteenth Edition of *The Bluebook* is the same as the Seventeenth Edition with regard to the meaning and use of signals.

What do these confusing rules and signals mean to practitioners? Consider the following tips:

- Review the signals set forth in Rule 1.2, and recognize that distinctions between some signals are nearly indecipherable.
- Use "no signal" when you are quoting or when the cited authority directly states the proposition.
- Use *see* when your authority clearly supports the statement you are making but requires an inferential step between the authority cited and the proposition it supports.
- When totally confused, consider using no signal and then discussing parenthetically the meaning of the authority cited, for example: *Parks v. Carter,* 432 P.2d 18, 20 (Cal. 1994) (holding that . . . .).

Presentation of Signals

Perhaps even more difficult than learning what *The Bluebook*'s signals mean is learning how to present the signals. Follow these guides:

- Capitalize the signal only if it begins a sentence. Otherwise, use a lowercase letter.
- Italicize or underscore signals when they are used in citation sentences or clauses (if the signal is two words, use a solid unbroken line, for example: See generally Paul S. Kaye, Blue Sky Law, 201 Mo. L. Rev. 118, 120 (1988)).
- When underscoring, separate the signal from an authority that is also underscored with a broken line, as follows: See Ford v. Hazard, 689 F.2d 118, 134 (9th Cir. 1990).

	Fifteenth Edition	Sixteenth Edition	Seventeenth Edition	Eighteenth Edition
[No signal]	Citation clearly states the proposition, identifies the source of a quotation, or identifies an authority referred to in text.	Citation identifies the source of a quotation or identifies an authority referred to in text.	Citation directly states the proposition, identifies the source of a quotation, or identifies an authority referred to in text.	Same as Seventeenth Edition.
See	Citation clearly supports the proposition.	Citation directly states or clearly supports the proposition.	Citation clearly supports the proposition.	Same as Seventeenth Edition.
Contra	Citation directly states the contrary of the proposition.	*Contra* signal did not exist in the Sixteenth Edition	Citation directly states the contrary of the proposition.	Same as Seventeenth Edition.

Figure 8-1   Chart Showing Changes in *Bluebook* Signals

- When combining the signal *see* with another signal such as *e.g.* (to indicate that other authorities also state or support the proposition, but giving their citations would not be particularly helpful), follow the word *see* with a comma, as follows: *See, e.g., Allen v. Riley*, 610 P.2d 118 (Or. 1997).
- Do not italicize or underscore the signal if you use the signal as an ordinary verb in a sentence rather than as a shorthand instruction to the reader. Thus, the following is correct: For a general discussion of deeds of trust, see 78 C.J.S. *Deeds and Conveyances* § 48 (1994).
- When using a variety of signals within a "string," note that Rule 1.3 imposes a hierarchy on their presentation, meaning they should be listed in the order in which they are presented in *The Bluebook* (namely, supporting signals, comparative signals, contradictory ones, and background ones). If there are two supporting signals, they should be separated from each other by semicolons. If those two signals are followed by a signal indicating contradiction, a new sentence should be started to show the new type of signal. An example is provided in Rule 1.3 of *The Bluebook*.
- Authorities within each signal are separated by semicolons and presented in the order given in Rule 1.4 (statutes listed before cases,

federal cases listed before state cases, cases from higher courts listed before cases from lower courts, and so forth).

Conclusion

The use of citation signals is frustrating even for the most practiced writers. Continually and carefully review their meanings. Reread Rule 1.2 several times so you can quickly and immediately convey to a reader the import of the authorities you cite. In the long run, mastering the citation signals will save you much time.

Related Authority (Rule 1.6)

On occasion, writers may wish to direct a reader to an authority related to or which discusses or quotes the specific authority cited. Such direction is accomplished through an italicized (or underscored) phrase that does not appear in parentheses. Commonly used directions include *quoted in, construed in, available at,* and *questioned in.* Use the following format: Hatch Act § 1, 36 U.S.C. § 50 (2000), *construed in James v. NRCC,* 520 U.S. 118, 126-27 (2004). If underscoring, use a solid unbroken line for the phrase, as follows: Linda Allen, Treble Damages in Antitrust Cases, 6 Duke L.J. 203 (1994), reprinted in Philip Hendrix, The Law of Antitrust 45 (3d ed. 1999).

Note that a parenthetical explanation that follows an authority and whose first word ends with the suffix "ing" (such as "quoting," "citing," or "construing") is not italicized or underscored, although phrases that introduce related authority (such as *quoted in* or *reprinted in*) are underscored or italicized. Thus, the following is correct: *Monument Sav. Bank v. Tyson Fed'n,* 504 U.S. 106, 109 (1997) (quoting *Draper v. Farrell,* 501 U.S. 19, 22 (1995)).

Capitalization (Rule 8; B10.6)

The Bluebook includes a number of rules relating to the capitalization of certain words. The most significant rules are as follows:

- Capitalize the "C" in Court:
  - ➤ Whenever you refer to the U.S. Supreme Court.
  - ➤ When referring to the court to which you are addressing a document or request (for example, always state "Plaintiff respectfully urges this Court to grant her Motion for Summary Judgment").

➤ When naming a specific court in full (as in the following: "The Eighth Circuit Court of Appeals clearly held that . . . .").

● Do not capitalize the "c" in "court" when you are discussing a court (other than the U.S. Supreme Court) in a general manner, such as follows: "The court in *Taylor* also held . . . .").

● Capitalize party identifications in the matter being adjudicated such as "Plaintiff," "Petitioner," or "Defendant," but not when they refer to parties in other actions, as follows: "The Defendant has asserted in his Answer that the action is barred by the statute of limitations. Plaintiff submits that Defendant has misinterpreted the position of the defendant in *Anderson*."

● Capitalize the first letter in each significant word in the title of a court document, such as the following: "In Plaintiff's Motion to Compel Answers to Interrogatories, Plaintiff argues that . . . ."

● Capitalize proper nouns referring to the Constitution or various acts, such as "First Amendment," "Bill of Rights," and "Gold Clause Act."

● Capitalize "circuit" only when referring to a particular circuit by name or number, such as in the following statement: "The Ninth Circuit ruled that . . . ."

● Capitalize the "J" in justice or judge when giving the name of a specific jurist or when referring to any U.S. Supreme Court Justice, as in "Justice Breyer" or "the Justice stated . . . ."

● Capitalize the word "state" when it is part of the full title of a state, as in "the State of Ohio."

Practice Tip

✓ While most writers have been taught to spell out the numbers one through nine and use figures for the numbers 10 and larger, *The Bluebook* position is quite different: *The Bluebook* instructs one to spell out the numbers zero to ninety-nine in text (Rule 6.2).

Additionally, *The Bluebook* states that one should use commas in numbers only when the number contains five or more digits (Rule 6.2). Thus, *The Bluebook* provides that one write, "There are 9876 pages in the transcript." Most writers would prefer to write, "There are 9,876 pages in the transcript."

Exercise for Chapter 8

A. Correct the following. Assume that each number to the left of a question refers to a page within a brief being submitted to a court in your state and that there are no intervening citations between questions. If alternative forms of citation are acceptable, give all. Assume the citations are "stand-alone" citations.

   1. *Peters v. Colonial General Partnership*, 134 F.3d 909, 913 (Fifth Circuit 1998).

   _____

   2. Refer to page 915 of the *Peters* case.

   _____

   3. Lynne M. Wagner, *Enterprise Law*, Section 101 (second edition 1994).

   _____

   4. Refer to section 120 of Ms. Wagner's book.

   _____

   5. Refer to page 920 of the *Peters* case.

   _____

   _____

   6. Refer to section 125 of Ms. Wagner's book.

   _____

B. Correct the following and describe the meaning of any signal used.

   1. But see *Edmonson v. Pearce*, 911 P. 2d 605 (Oklahoma 1993).

   _____

   _____

2. E.g. *Sisler v. TRS Advertising & Marketing Co.*, 809 F. Supp. 2d 18 (District court Connecticut 1999).

_____

_____

3. For additional discussion of this topic, see Judith M. Schillings, *Land Use Concepts,* Journal of Land Use and Environmental Law, volume 109, page 166 (2000).

_____

_____

C. Correct the following statements made in a brief submitted to a court.

The plaintiff in this case has vigorously asserted that her rights under the fourth amendment to the U.S. constitution have been violated. When the police officers employed by the state of California entered her home, they did so without a warrant. Warrantless searches are clear violations not only of the fourth amendment but also of California's Tempesta act. The judicial branch of the Federal Government has repeatedly upheld the rights of citizens to be protected in their own homes. As justice Anthony Kennedy of the U.S. Supreme Court has commented, "There is no greater right than that of our citizens to be protected from government intrusion in their homes." Therefore, plaintiff respectfully urges this court to grant her motion to dismiss all charges against her.

9 Putting It Together

■ The Table of Authorities

Many documents need (and court rules may require) a table of the authorities cited in the document. The table is presented at or near the beginning of the document or brief. A table of authorities lists each authority cited in a brief (whether in text or footnotes) together with a reference to the page or pages of the document on which each appears so that readers can readily locate a discussion of specific cases or other authorities. While *The Bluebook* gives hundreds of pages of information about isolated citations, it provides no direction whatsoever as to setting up a table of authorities. Thus, comply with court rules (if they exist) or your firm or office practices (if they exist). Failing any direction, consider the following:

- Although many word processing programs and Lexis's FullAuthority and Westlaw's WestCheck will automatically extract citations from your document and create a table of authorities, some individuals still prefer to use the "old-fashioned" approach: listing each authority in a separate document or on an index card and then "shuffling" them until they are in the right order.
- Citations that appear in a table of authorities are literally "standalone" citations (in that they appear by themselves rather than in a textual sentence), which would thus, per Table T.6 of *The Bluebook*, allow for abbreviation of words in a case name, such as "Bankruptcy,"

"Development," and "Society." Nevertheless, most practitioners prefer not to abbreviate such words in the table of authorities, and only abbreviate widely known acronyms and the eight words listed in Rule 10.2.1(c), such as "Co." and "Corp.," so that the table, often the first substantive part of a brief reviewed by a reader, has a formal, complete, and professional appearance.

- If you decide to use full case names rather than treating the citations in the table as "stand alones," as discussed previously, be especially careful when allowing a word processing program to create your table. If on page 6 of your brief, for example, you refer to "*Cooley Agric. Bd. v. Redmond Indem. Co.*, 15 F. Supp. 2d 18 (D.N.J. 1998)," some word processing programs will recreate the citation in your table exactly in that form, requiring you to manually convert the citation to "*Cooley Agriculture Board v. Redmond Indemnity Co.*, 15 F. Supp. 2d 18 (D.N.J. 1998)" for the table of authorities. Whichever method you select, be consistent. Don't show *Adams v. American Communications Co.* and then *Bailey v. Aetna Cas. & Sur. Co.*

- Group your citations together according to the type of authority. For example, first list all the cases together under the heading "Cases," then all of the statutes under the heading "Statutes," then all of the miscellaneous authorities, and so forth. If your brief consists mainly of cases with only a few other authorities, your table will likely have just two categories: "Cases" and "Other Authorities." List primary authorities before you list secondary authorities. Remember that unless court rules require a certain organization, there are no rigid rules regarding preparation of tables of authorities. Consider the reader, and use a presentation that readily communicates information. Some writers follow Rule 1.4 relating to the order of citations in strings as a guideline to the order of citations for a table of authorities.

- Within each grouping, list authorities alphabetically (listing cases alphabetically by plaintiff, such that the *Baker* case appears before the *Franklin* case which appears before the *Jacobs* case); by ascending number (such that 15 U.S.C. § 2041 (2000) appears before 15 U.S.C. § 2049 (2000), which appears before 18 U.S.C. § 101 (2000)); or by author's name (such that an article by Thomas Howard is listed before one by Christopher Walter).

- Do not include introductory signals (such as *see*) or parenthetical expressions (such as "explaining that . . . .").

- Include subsequent history of a citation (such as *cert. denied* or *aff'd*) inasmuch as it is part of the full citation.

- Omit pinpoint citations in the table of authorities.
- Ensure that each time an authority is mentioned (whether in text or footnotes), the table reflects such. Thus, if your brief includes a reference to a certain case on page 4, and then there is an *id.* reference to the same case on page 5, and a later short form reference to the same case on page 11, the table should reflect that the case is discussed on pages 4, 5, and 11.
- Use *passim* rather than listing each page on which the authority appears if you cite a certain authority on numerous occasions throughout the document.
- Always double-check the table of authorities to ensure that if the table says a certain authority is discussed on pages 10 and 14 of your brief, it is discussed on those pages.

Practice Tip

✓ How does one alphabetize a case name such as *In re Lowrey*? Is it alphabetized under "I" or under "L" as *In re Lowrey*? Unfortunately, there is no good answer to this question. Books of case reports such as *Federal Supplement* alphabetize such cases by the first letter of the party's name, as in *Lowrey, In re;* however, that may be for ease of retrieval when there are numerous cases in the book that begin with the phrase *In re.* A review of briefs filed with the U.S. Supreme Court shows some variation, but most briefs show such cases alphabetized under "I" and presented as follows:

Hunter v. Amoco Products Co.
In re Lowe
In re Peterson
Jackson v. Phillips

Other briefs would place *In re Peterson* with the "P" cases, although they would continue to show it in the table as *In re Peterson*.

Alphabetize cases in which the United States is a party under "U" as in *United States v. Georgia* and then *United States v. Munoz*.

When in doubt, review briefs filed with the U.S. Supreme
Court at the Court's website at http://www.supremecourtus.gov
to get ideas about setting up tables of authorities.

■ Footnotes

Many legal writers prefer to cite their authorities in footnotes rather than in
the narrative portion of the text. Other writers use both techniques in the
same document, placing some authorities in the text of the document and
others in footnotes. Endnotes (listing all authorities on a separate page at
the end of a document) are rarely, if ever, used by legal writers (except in
textbooks).

There are two schools of thought on the use of footnotes. Some writers
believe that using citations throughout the narrative is distracting and,
thus, placing the citations in footnotes facilitates uninterrupted reading
of a document. Other writers believe exactly the opposite, reasoning that
when readers encounter a footnote either they train themselves to ignore it
(in which case, the footnote is of no value) or, indulging a natural curiosity,
they jump from the narrative to the footnote to see what it says, thus
interrupting the flow of the argument.

Some courts have rules regarding or even prohibiting the citation of
authorities in footnotes (realizing that typeface in footnotes is often smaller
than that used in the narrative portion of text, thus allowing writers to
squeeze more material into a brief and perhaps exceed page limits), and
others limit the number of footnotes that may be used. Review these rules,
and consult with colleagues in your office to determine if one practice is
more favored than another.

If citing authorities in footnotes, consider the following:

● Because footnotes in and of themselves can be distracting, do not
   distract readers further by appending excessive substantive explanatory parentheticals to cases cited. For example, avoid the following
   approach: "[1] *Dyer v. Maxwell*, 904 F.2d 118, 130-34 (9th Cir. 1994)
   (holding that abandonment of a trademark is presumed to have
   occurred after three years, although the presumption can be over-
   come by clear and convincing evidence otherwise, such as occurs
   when the trademark owner has made use of the mark customary

in its trade or profession, so long as that use is not merely a token use)." If an issue merits substantive discussion, it likely merits discussion in the body of the work. Moreover, some readers have trained themselves to ignore footnotes, believing information therein is likely to be extraneous to the main argument. Thus, making key arguments in footnotes may well be futile.

- Avoid footnotes that continue or "wrap" from one page to the next. For example, consider a reader who is reviewing page four of a brief and encounters a footnote. The reader glances down at the bottom of page four, begins reading the footnote, and must continue on to pages five and six to finish reading the footnote. When finished reading the footnote, the reader must return to page four and remember where he or she left off. Such a style is terribly distracting for almost all readers. Some will not return to the original page, thus missing significant portions of an analysis.

- If there are several citations within one footnote, the use of *id.* in that footnote will send a reader to the immediately preceding authority within that same footnote. Alternatively, *id.* can be used as a footnote to refer to a preceding separate footnote, as long as there is only one authority cited within that preceding footnote. In brief, *id.* may be used when the preceding citation contains only one source.

- If you are directing a reader to a footnote within a source you cite, indicate as follows: "Harry S. Hunter, Annotation, *Tobacco Litigation,* 78 A.L.R.4th 106, 108 n.14 (1996)." (See Rule 3.2(b).) Note that there is no space between the "n." and the footnote reference. Cite multiple footnotes as follows: "nn.343-47."

Practice Tip

✓ There are three separate references in the Bluepages of *The Bluebook* that suggest that practitioners do not use footnotes in their writings:

- B2 (page 3) states that citations are inserted into the text.
- B8.2 (page 18) provides in part, "Since you will not be using footnote citations...."

- B13 (page 24) provides that "[c]itations appear within the text of the document."

Thus, *The Bluebook* position is that while those writing law review articles and journals will place citations in footnotes, practitioners place their citations in the narrative text of a document. Nevertheless, many practitioners use footnotes (usually in combination with citations in the text of a document), and they will likely continue to do so, despite *The Bluebook* position.

■ Internal Cross-References (Rule 3.5)

If you wish to send a reader to another part of the brief or document itself, be as specific as possible. Although there is nothing prohibiting you from merely directing the reader, "See Section III, *supra*," it is easier for the reader if you provide the exact page, as follows: "See Section III, *supra* p. 8." This directs the reader to page 8 within your document to review Section III. Note that "p." and "pp." (for "pages") are used only for internal cross-references.

As discussed in Chapter 8, although *The Bluebook* does not require it, many authors prefer to tell readers where in the brief they can locate previously cited authorities. For example, if you cite a book by Charles Grant on page two of your brief, then you discuss and cite a variety of other authorities, and then on page six you again cite Charles Grant's book, you may do so as follows: "Grant, *supra* p. 2, at 909" (directing the reader to return to page two of your brief and then to review page 909 of Charles Grant's book).

If you are directing a reader to a previous footnote within your brief, follow the format: "Grant, *supra* note 23, at 909" (directing the reader to return to footnote number 23 in your brief and then to review page 909 of Charles Grant's book).

Remember that when directing a reader to pages or notes within your brief, *supra* is not followed by a comma (as in "Grant, *supra* note 23, at 909"). When directing a reader to a page within the previously cited authority, *supra* is followed by a comma (as in "Grant, *supra*, at 909").

Practice Tip

✓ Because the addition or deletion of any material from your document will likely cause changes in pagination, insert the internal cross-reference page numbers only when the document is near completion. Use blank lines as you prepare the document, then replace them with actual page numbers just before final typing. Alternatively, you can use a unique combination of letters (perhaps your initials or XOX) instead of blank lines, then use the "find" and "replace" functions on your word processor to replace these initials with the actual page numbers.

■ Final Tasks in Cite-Checking

Before any document that includes citations leaves your office, take the following last steps to ensure the document is accurate:

- Proofread carefully to ensure typists or word processors correctly made the revisions you requested.
- Be alert to inconsistency. If you underscored case names, then book titles and signals should be similarly underscored. Ensure that the document does not flip back and forth between underscoring and italicizing, which can easily occur if more than one author has worked on the document.
- Make sure the final document is printed by one printer because the use of different printers can result in a different appearance among pages.
- Recheck all of the short form signals, such as *id.* and *supra*. If material has either been added to or deleted from a document, these signals may well be incorrect.
- Check the accuracy of each quotation. Quotations must be reproduced scrupulously. If changes are made, make sure they are indicated through the use of ellipses or bracketed information.
- Check to make sure pinpoints are included for all citations.

- Review the table of authorities to ensure that all case names are full and complete (with only commonly known acronyms and words such as "Inc." and "Corp." abbreviated) if this is your office practice and that the references to the pages in the document on which authorities appear are correct. Do not rely exclusively on word processing programs to reproduce the table. Do your own proofreading.

Exercise for Chapter 9

Use a separate sheet of paper to create a table of authorities for the following authorities that will be cited in a brief. You may need to supply missing information, and make corrections in and additions to the citations. You need not provide a reference to pages on which these authorities would appear in the brief.

Dura Pharmaceuticals, Inc. v. Broudo, 539 US 909 (2004)

Carden v. Arkoma Association, 494 U.S. 185

James R. Michaels, *Normative Constructions*, 190, 195 (2d ed. 1994)

Temple v. Synthes Corporation, 130 F. 3d 18 (3rd Cir. 2001)

United States of America v. BestFoods, Inc., 524 U.S. 51 (1998)

17 U.S.C. § 109

17 U.S.C. § 100

American Car & Foundry Co. v. Kettelhake, 236 U.S. 311 (1915)

28 U.S.C. § 1332

28 U.S.C. § 1332(a)

Hanover Star Construction Co. v. Metcalf Communications, 114 F. Supp. 2d 90 (S.D. Ca. 1996)

14 B Charles Alan Wright and Arthur R. Miller, *Federal Practice and Procedure* § 110 (3d edition 1998)

John B. Oakley, *Prospectus for the American Law Institute's Federal Judicial Code Revision Project,* 31 U.C. Davis Law Rev. 990 (1998)

Lumberman's Mutual Casualty Co. v. Elbert, 348 U.S. 48 (1954)

Maine Revised Statutes Annotated, title 19, § 909

10 The Final Review

Correct the citations in the following brief and memorandum. The brief is based on an actual brief filed by the U.S. Department of Justice and was revised (and condensed) to provide a "real life" example of a court brief. The author wishes to apologize to the authors of the original brief for these revisions and changes.

You may need to create information such as dates and pinpoints. Follow *Bluebook* rules.

IN THE UNITED STATES DISTRICT COURT FOR THE DISTRICT OF COLUMBIA

UNITED STATES OF AMERICA,

      Plaintiff,

      v.   Civil Action No. 98-1232 (TPJ)

MICROSOFT CORPORATION,

      Defendant.

STATE OF NEW YORK *ex rel.*
Attorney General ELIOT SPITZER, *et al.*,

Plaintiffs,

v.   Civil Action No. 98-1233 (TPJ)

MICROSOFT CORPORATION

Defendants.

Plaintiffs' Response to Microsoft's Objection to Participation by Professor Lawrence Lessig as an Amicus Curiae

Microsoft has objected to participation by Professor Lawrence Lessig of Harvard Law School as an amicus curiae. Professor Lessig's participation in that role is proper, and Microsoft's objections are ill conceived and unfounded.

I. Background

By Order dated November 19, 1999, the court invited Professor Lessig to participate as amicus curiae. The Court also permitted the two plaintiffs and Microsoft each to designate an amicus curiae. In a conference with counsel the day before its Order, the Court explained that it asked Professor Lessig to submit a brief that addresses the legal issue of technological tying. (Transcript 10-11, November 18, 1999). The Court's Order followed the entry of the Court's detailed findings of fact. There is no suggestion in Microsoft's papers, nor could there be, that the amicus process has anything to do with issues of fact.

II. Legal Standard

Although there is no federal rule or statute governing participation by amicus curiae at the district court level, *see U.S. v. Gotti*, 755 F.Supp. 1157 (E.D.N.Y. 1991), a federal district court has the inherent authority to invite participation by amicus curiae to assist the court in its proceedings. *United States v. Louisiana*, 751 F. Supp. 608, 620 (E.D. La. 1990). *United States v. Michigan*, 807 Fed. Supp. 655, 660 (W. Dist. Mich. 1987). The decision to invite or accept participation by an amicus is committed to the sound discretion of the court. *Allen v. Hall*, 776 F.Supp. 152 (D.S.C. 1974).

The classic role of the amicus curiae is to assist in a case of general public interest, supplement the efforts of counsel, and draw the court's attention to law that may otherwise escape consideration. *Miller-Wohl Co. v. Commissioner of Labor & Industry*, 694 F.2d 203, 204 (9th Cir. 1982); *see also New England Patriots Football Club, Inc. v. University of Chi.*, 592 F.2d 1196, 1198 n.3 (1st Cir. 1979) (noting that historically, the role of an amicus was "to aid the court in resolving doubtful issues of law"). There is no requirement that an amicus be disinterested. *Funbus Sys., Inc. v. California Public Utilities Comm'n*, 801 F.2d 1120, 1125 (9th Cir. 1986); *Hoptowit v. Ray*, 682 F.2d 1237, 1260 (9th Cir. 1982). In this case there is no reason to believe that Professor Lessig is other than disinterested.

III. Argument

A. Microsoft's Arguments

First, Microsoft asserts, without any explanation of its foundation or reasoning, that the Court's Order inviting Professor Lessig's participation is sufficiently broad to constitute a request for proposed conclusions of law. Microsoft also contends that Professor Lessig does not meet requirements to participate as an amicus because he does not have a "particularized 'special interest'" in the legal issues presented in the case but then goes on to argue, seemingly paradoxically, that he should not participate because he is not impartial. (Def.'s Opposition to Order ¶12, Nov. 20, 1999.) These objections are specious.

B. Role of Amicus Curiae

"Amicus curiae" is a Latin phrase for "friend of the court" and an amicus curiae is to be distinguished from an advocate before the court. *Allen, supra.* Traditionally, an amicus curiae was a neutral provider of information or legal insight to the court, and if partisan, amicus curiae status would be denied. However, the trend, particularly in appellate courts, is to accept and even invite the participation of amici curiae with partisan interests. 4 Am. Jur. 2d *Amicus Curiae* § 6 (1986).

In fact, modern courts have consistently recognized the role of amicus curiae as partisans.

> "We recognize that the acceptance of amicus briefs is within the sound discretion of the court, and that by the nature of things an amicus is not normally impartial. Furthermore, if an amicus causes the district court to make an error of law — an amicus who argues facts should rarely be welcomed — the error can be corrected on appeal. Nonetheless, we believe a district court lacking joint consent of the parties should go slow in accepting, and even slower in inviting, an amicus brief unless, as a party, although short of a right to intervene, the amicus has a special interest that justifies his

having a say, or unless the court feels that existing counsel may need supplementing assistance." *Strasser v. Doorley*, 432 F.2d 567, 569 (1st Cir. 1970).

C. Legal Argument by Amici Will Not Usurp the Judicial Function

That Professor Lessig and the other potential amici may discuss how they believe that the Sherman Act, 15 U.S.C. §§ 1-6212, should be applied to the facts as the Court has found them is neither unusual nor improper, and indeed is the traditional role of an amicus. *See e.g., Funbus*, 801 F.2d at 1125, in which the court noted that it is perfectly permissible for amicus to "take a legal position and present legal arguments in support of it." Submitting a brief as amici involves *no* delegation of judicial authority or duties and is unobjectionable.

D. If the Court Believes That Professor Lessig Would Bring a Helpful Perspective to Legal Issues in the Case, It Is Appropriate for Him to Participate as Amicus

"There are no strict prerequisites that must be established prior to qualifying for amicus status; an individual seeking to appear as amicus must merely make a showing that his participation is useful or otherwise desirable by the court. *United States*, 751 F. Supp. at 620. Although some courts have required that the amicus possess some "unique information or perspective," *see Ryan v. Commodity Futures Trading Comm'n*, 125 F.3d 1062 (7th Cir. 1997), this does not require any particular quantum of expertise beyond the expectation that the amicus will add significantly to, not merely parrot, the contributions from the lawyers for the parties. Moreover, the court in Gotti, 755 F. Supp. at 1158-1159, rejected a proffered amicus brief that merely parroted the arguments of the defendants in that case.

E. Microsoft Has Not Demonstrated That Professor Lessig Is Biased Against It

When Microsoft first raised the issue of Professor Lessig's purposed bias, this Court found that Microsoft's bases for its allegations were "both trivial and altogether non-probative." (Memorandum & Order 2, Jan. 14, 1998.) In any event, there is no requirement that an amicus be impartial or disinterested. *Hoptowit*, 682 F.2d at 1260; Krislov, Samuel, *The Amicus Curiae Brief: From Friendship to Advocacy*, 72 Yale Law J. 694 (1963). Indeed, "by the nature of things an amicus is not normally disinterested." *Strasser*, 432 F.2d at 569. According to at least one expert, "an amicus brief is rarely disinterested;

usually it supports one party or the other." Michael Tigar, *Federal Appeals: Jurisdiction and Practice* 133 (2nd Ed. 1993). Therefore, Professor Lessig's participation as an amicus curiae is proper.

IV. Conclusion

For the foregoing reasons, the plaintiffs submit that it is entirely proper and appropriate for the court to invite Professor Lessig to participate as amicus curiae in this case of public importance.

Dated: _____

Respectfully submitted,

_____

MEMORANDUM

To: Francis M. Sullivan
From: Rita Lopez
Re: Liability of Grace Pattersen for Dog Bite
Date: August 18

Factual Background

Our client, Phil Franklin ("Franklin") lives in a residential neighborhood in California. His next-door neighbor is Grace Pattersen ("Pattersen"), who owns a large German shepherd dog, which has previously nipped at a neighborhood child. Two weeks ago, Franklin entered Pattersen's yard and approached Pattersen's door to deliver some mail that inadvertently came to Franklin's house. When Franklin approached the door, he bent down to greet the dog. The dog came out of the unlocked front door and bit Franklin. Franklin received several stitches for the dog bite.

Analysis

Introduction

While many jurisdictions previously followed the view that a dog was allowed "one free bite," this theory has waned as jurisdictions have adopted statutes that impose strict or absolute liability on dog owners for the acts of their dogs. Ward Miller, *Modern Status of Rule of Absolute or Strict Liability for Dogbite*, 51

A.L.R.4th 446, 452 (2000). In fact, California has enacted such a statute. Cal. Civil Code § 3342. That statute provides, in pertinent part, as follows:

> "The owner of any dog is liable for the damages suffered by any person who is bitten by the dog while . . . lawfully in a private place, including the property of the owner of the dog, regardless of the former viciousness of the dog or the owner's knowledge of such viciousness. A person is lawfully upon the private property of such owner . . . when he is on such property upon the invitation, express or implied, of the owner.

Thus, if Franklin was lawfully on Pattersen's property within the meaning of the statute, Pattersen is strictly liable for the injuries inflicted by her dog whether or not the dog previously displayed any viciousness and whether or not Pattersen knew of such viciousness.

Implied Invitees

One of the key issues in this case is whether Franklin was lawfully on Pattersen's property as an invitee. Franklin was not expressly invited onto Pattersen's property, so the issue is whether he was an implied invitee. The effect of the portion of the statute to exclude its protections to one who is not lawfully on the dog owner's property lawfully is to deny liability to trespassers. *Fullerton v. Conan*, 197 P.2d 59, 63 (Cal. App. 1948).

The term "invitee" is often construed broadly. For example, an invitation may be implied from customary use or manifested by the conduct of the parties. 61 Am. Jur. 2d, Premises Liability § 94 (1986). Similarly, the status of a person as an invitee often depends upon circumstances such as custom or the habitual acquiescence of the property owner. *Id.* Moreover, Restatement (2d) of Torts § 167 (1986) provides that consent to enter another's land can be derived from the relationship of the parties, as is the case with friends, social visitors, or business visitors.

In *Smythe v. Schacht*, 209 P.2d 114 (Cal. 1949), the court found that a child who entered the defendant's property to greet the defendant's son and was thereafter bitten by the defendant's son was on the premises with defendant's implied invitation. The children were playmates and the victim had previously entered the premises on other occasions. Thus, the child was lawfully on the premises.

In the present case, Franklin entered Pattersen's property for the sole purpose of delivering her mail. Social custom and courtesy would dictate that a neighbor deliver misdirected mail. Thus, it seems clear that Franklin was on Pattersen's property with her implied invitation.

Defenses

In adopting its dog-bite statute, California did not intend to eliminate defenses such as assumption of the risk. *Gomes v. Byrne*, 333 P.2d 754 (Cal.). Assumption of the risk requires that a person must know and appreciate the danger involved in an activity and yet voluntarily accept that risk. *Prescott v. Ralph's Grocery Co.*, 265 P.2d 904, 906-907 (Cal. 1954). Similarly, victims are denied recovery in dog-bite cases when they intentionally provoke or tease a dog that then bites them. Miller, *supra*, at 455.

In *Gomes*, 333 P.2d at 755, a salesman approached a yard enclosed by a fence and was followed along the fence by a dog which had barked at him for 50 feet. When the salesman opened the gate and entered the yard, he was bitten by the defendant's dog. The court held that while a person must have actual knowledge of a risk to be denied recovery, such knowledge may be inferred from the circumstances. *Supra* at 756. Because the salesman knew of the dog's hostility and yet voluntarily exposed himself to an obvious hazard, he assumed the risk of being bitten. Id. In the present case, Franklin was bitten immediately after Pattersen's door was opened. These facts are clearly distinguishable from those in *Gomes*, in which the salesman had observed a hostile, barking dog and yet chose to enter the owner's land.

Conclusion

Franklin was likely an implied invitee of Pattersen's because he entered her land for the purpose of fulfilling a social courtesy. Moreover, he neither provoked the dog nor did he have actual knowledge of the dog's aggressive nature. In such a case, he will be afforded the protection of California Civil Code section 3342, and Pattersen will have strict liability for the actions of her dog.

Answer Keys

When italics are used in the answer keys, underscoring is also proper.

Exercise for Chapter 2

The following are examples found in **The Bluebook.** *Correct them for use by practitioners.*

1. MODEL BUS. CORP. ACT § 57 (1979).
   Model Bus. Corp. Act § 57 (1979).

2. U.S. CONST. art. IV, § 1.
   U.S. Const. art. IV, § 1.

3. N.Y. BUS. CORP. LAW § 717 (McKinney 2003).
   N.Y. Bus. Corp. Law § 717 (McKinney 2003).

4. BLACK'S LAW DICTIONARY 712 (7th ed. 1999).
   Black's Law Dictionary 712 (7th ed. 1999).

5. David Rudovsky, *Police Abuse: Can the Violence Be Contained?*, 27 HARV. C.R.-C.L. L. REV. 465, 500 (1992).
   David Rudovsky, *Police Abuse: Can the Violence Be Contained?*, 27 Harv. C.R.-C.L. Rev. 465, 500 (1992).

6. H.R. REP. NO. 99-253, pt. 1, at 54 (1985).
   H.R. Rep. No. 99-253, pt. 1, at 54 (1985).

7. FED. R. CIV. P. 11.
Fed. R. Civ. P. 11.

Exercise for Chapter 3

Correct the following citations. You may need to supply or create missing information. There may be more than one thing wrong with the citation. You do not need to include pinpoint citations in the answers. (Note that case names and signals may be either underscored or italicized.)

Case Names

1. Tracy Singer versus A.M. Kimball
Singer v. Kimball

2. T.N. Andrews, III, Vs. Blake Ellison, James Gray, and Leon Nelson
Andrews v. Ellison

3. Commonwealth of Virginia V. Talbot Chemical Department (Assume the citation appears as a "stand-alone" citation.)
Commonwealth v. Talbot Chem. Dep't

4. USA v. Reynolds Building Federation Incorporated (Cite first assuming citation appears in a textual sentence, and then cite as a stand-alone citation.)
United States v. Reynolds Building Federation Inc. (in textual sentence)
United States v. Reynolds Bldg. Fed'n Inc. (in stand-alone citation)

5. Helen and Delia Parry versus Securities and Exchange Commission
Parry v. SEC (per Rule 6.1(b), *Parry v. Securities & Exchange Commission* is also correct, but the first form is preferred.)

State Court Cases

6. Forras v. Hecker, 309 Massachusetts 601 (Assume citation appears in a brief submitted to a court requiring parallel citations.)
Forras v. Hecker, 309 Mass. 601, xxx N.E.2d xxx (19xx).

7. Douglas v. Dixon, 201 Cal. 3rd 990, 89 California Reporter 14, 909 Pacific Reporter (Second Series) 292 (2003). (Assume the citation appears in a brief submitted to a court requiring parallel citations.)
Douglas v. Dixon, 201 Cal. 3d 990, 909 P.2d 292, 89 Cal. Rptr. 14 (2003).

8. Douglas v. Dixon, 201 Cal. 3rd 990, 89 California Reporter 14, 909 Pacific Reporter (Second Series) 292 (2003). (Assume the citation appears in a brief submitted to a court that does not require parallel citations.)
Douglas v. Dixon, 909 P.2d 292 (Cal. 2003).

9. Smithson v. Garcia, an Indiana Supreme Court case decided in 2000.
Smithson v. Garcia, xxx N.E.2d xxx (Ind. 2000).

10. United States v. Nordic Village, Inc., a 2004 Indiana court of appeals case (Assume the citation appears as a stand-alone citation).
United States v. Nordic Vill. Inc., xxx N.E.2d xxx (Ind. Ct. App. 2004).

Federal Cases and Subsequent History

11. Jeffrey v. Cross Country Bank, 530 United States Reports 616, 214 Supreme Court Reporter 144, 210 Lawyers Edition, Second Series, 995 (2001).
Jeffrey v. Cross Country Bank, 530 U.S. 616 (2001).

12. Hornbuckle v. State Farm Lloyds, a 2006 Fifth Circuit case located at volume 385 of the Federal Reporter, Third Series, at page 538. (Assume *certiorari* was denied for this case by the United States Supreme Court in 2006).
Hornbuckle v. State Farm Lloyds, 385 F.3d 538 (5th Cir. 2006), *cert. denied,* xxx U.S. xxx (2007).

13. Bains LLC v. Arco Products Co., 405 F. 3d 764 (2003). (Assume this case was affirmed by the United States Supreme Court in 2005).
Bains LLC v. Arco Products Co., 405 F.3d 764 (xxx Cir. 2003), *aff'd,* xxx U.S. xxx (2005).
(Note: *Products* may appear as *Prods.* if citation appears as a stand-alone. Note that answer must include some reference to a circuit court of appeals.)

14. Charter Company v. Riggs Bank of Washington, D.C., 23 Federal Supplement, Second Series, page 119.
Charter Co. v. Riggs Bank, 23 F. Supp. 2d 119 (D.D.C. 2000).
(Note: Other district court abbreviations and other dates are acceptable. Also, "of Washington, D.C." may be included if it is the entity's full name.)

15. Alvaro v. Gustin, a case from the Southern District of New York, decided in 2005 and reversed by the Second Circuit Court of Appeals in 2005. *Alvaro v. Gustin,* xxx F. Supp. 2d xxx (S.D.N.Y.), *rev'd,* xxx F.3d xxx (2d Cir. 2005).

Spacing

16. 38 Federal Reporter (Third Series) 107.
    38 F.3d 107.

17. 402 New York Reports, Second Series, page 607.
    402 N.Y.2d 607.

18. Sullivan v. Sullivan, 526 United States Reports 111 (2003).
    Sullivan v. Sullivan, 526 U.S. 111 (2003).

19. Aztec Inc. v. Zodiac Co., 206 West Virginia Reports 114, 761 South Eastern Reporter (Second Series) 877 (2002).
    Aztec Inc. v. Zodiac Co., 206 W. Va. 114, 761 S.E.2d 877 (2002).

20. 47 New York University Law Review 26 (2000).
    47 N.Y.U. L. Rev. (2000).

21. 27 South Carolina Law Review 207 (2001).
    27 S.C. L. Rev. 207 (2001).

Exercise for Chapter 4

Correct the following citations. You may need to supply missing information.

1. Fourth Amendment to the U.S. Constitution.
   U.S. Const. amend. IV.

2. Article 3, Section 2, clause 1 of the U.S. Constitution.
   U.S. Const. art. III, § 2, cl.1.

3. Article VI of the California Constitution.
   Cal. Const. art. VI.

4. House of Representatives bill number 798, 108th Congress.
   H.R. 798, 108th Cong. § x (20xx).
                        or
   H.R. 798, 108th Cong. (20xx).

5. Statement of Senator Susan Collins, volume 142 of the Congressional Record, at page 169.
    142 Cong. Rec. 169 (year) (statement of Sen. Collins) or (statement of Sen. Susan Collins) [Note: *The Bluebook* shows both first and last names of speakers and last names only. See pages 117 and 118.]

6. The Patent Reform Act of 2005: Hearing on House of Representatives Bill No. 2795 before the House Subcommittee on Courts, the Internet, and Intellectual Property, held during the 109th Congress, Statement of Larry Ellison, Chief Executive Officer of Oracle Corporation.
    The Patent Reform Act of 2005: Hearing on H.R. 2795 Before the H. Subcomm. on Courts, the Internet, and Intellectual Property, 109th Cong. xx (20xx) (statement of Larry Ellison, Chief Executive Officer, Oracle Corp.)

7. Title 17, Section 106 of the United States Code.
    17 U.S.C. § 106 (2000).

8. Section 401 of Title 42 of United States Code Annotated. (Assume the statute is found only in the pocket part.)
    42 U.S.C. § 401 (West. Supp. year)

9. 11 United States Code Service Sections 507 through 517 (2003).
    11 U.S.C.S. §§ 507-517 (LexisNexis 2003).

10. Rhode Island General Law § 13-30-12.
    R. I. Gen. Laws § 13-30-12 (year)

11. Arizona Revised Statute Annotated Section 19 104 (West).
    Ariz. Rev. Stat. Ann. § 19-104 (year).

12. New York General Associations Law Sections 8709-8711.
    N.Y. Gen. Ass'ns Law §§ 8709-8711 (McKinney year) or
    N.Y. Gen. Ass'ns Law §§ 8709-8711 (Consol. year) or
    N.Y. Gen. Ass'ns Law §§ 8709-8711 (Gould year).

13. California Public Utilities Section 989.
    Cal. Pub. Util. § 989 (West year) or
    Cal. Pub. Util. § 989 (Deering year).

14. Uniform Commercial Code Section 3-216.
    U.C.C. § 3-216 (year).

15. Federal Rule of Civil Procedure 12(b)(6).
    Fed. R. Civ. P. 12(b)(6).

16. House of Representatives Report Number 108-04, page 62.
    H.R. Rep. No. 108-04, at 62 (year).

Exercise for **Chapter 5**

Correct the following citations. You may need to supply missing information.

1. The definition of "guardian" appearing on page 440 of Black's Law Dictionary, Eighth Edition, 2004.
Black's Law Dictionary 440 (8th ed. 2004).

2. Volume 7 of the second edition of a book written by Taylor R. Young, Jr., entitled "Health Care Law," sections 27 through 30.
7 Taylor R. Young, Jr., *Health Care Law* §§ 27-30 (2d ed. year).

3. A law review article appearing at page 919 of volume 43 of the Boston College Law Review, entitled "Gender and Social Policy" and written by Laura M. Hays.
Laura M. Hays, *Gender and Social Policy,* 43 B.C. L. Rev. 919 (year).

4. A discussion of Section 38 of the topic Venue in American Jurisprudence, Second Series, Volume 99.
99 Am. Jur. 2d *Venue* § 38 (year).

5. A 2004 book written by Stephen Bourne and Samuel Tarrant entitled "Securities Regulation," Section 409.
Stephen Bourne & Samuel Tarrant, *Securities Regulation* § 409 (2004).

6. A law review article published in volume 31 (page 909) of the Northern Kentucky Law Review in 2004, entitled "Mandatory Sentencing Guidelines," and written by Stephanie Wilkie-Harris.
Stephanie   Wilkie-Harris,   *Mandatory   Sentencing   Guidelines,* 31 N. Ky. L. Rev. 909 (2004).

7. An annotation entitled "Judicial Restraint" appearing in A.L.R. Fifth Series in 2004 and written by James J. Butler, IV.
James J. Butler, IV, Annotation, *Judicial Restraint,* xxx A.L.R.5th xxx (2004).

8. Restatement of Torts, Second Series, Section 39.
Restatement (Second) of Torts § 39 (year).

9. Section 19, comment b of the Restatement of Trusts, Second Series.
Restatement (Second) of Trusts § 19 cmt. b (year)
(Note: See Rule 12.8.5 for citations to comments.)

10. A November 2004 article written in the Tax Lawyer at page 49 by Cynthia Ann Gonzalez, entitled "Tax Reform: The New Code."
Cynthia Ann Gonzalez, *Tax Reform: The New Code,* xxx Tax Law. 49 (2004).
(Note: Per Rule 16.4, if this work appears in a periodical that is separately paginated within each issue, the form would be as follows: Cynthia Ann Gonzalez, *Tax Reform: The New Code,* Tax Law., Nov. 2004, at 49.)

Exercise for Chapter 6

Correct each citation. You may need to supply or create missing information. Assume citations are "stand-alone" citations. (Note: Per B10.2, citations to court documents should be enclosed in parentheses.)

1. Defendant's deposition, taken on April 14, 2005, at page 109.
(Def.'s Dep. 109: xx-xx, Apr. 14, 2005.)

2. Plaintiff's response to defendant's interrogatory number 32.
(Pl.'s Resp. to Def.'s Interrog. # 32.)

3. Exhibit F.
(Ex. F.)

4. Paragraph 14 of Defendant's Counterclaim.
(Def.'s Countercl. ¶ 14.)

5. Plaintiffs' Motion to Dismiss, paragraphs 21-31.
(Pls.' Mot. to Dismiss ¶¶ 21-31.)

6. *Laughlin v. Kmart Corp.,* volume 3, Blue Sky Law Reports, Paragraph 13, District Court of New Jersey, August 12, 2003).
Laughlin v. Kmart Corp., 3 Blue Sky L. Rep. (CCH) ¶ 13 (D.N.J. Aug. 12, 2003) (Note: Per Rule 19.1, if this case appears in a bound volume, include only the year 2003 in the parenthetical with the court information.)

7. Presidential Proclamation Number 7918. (Assume the material is not available in C.F.R.)
Proclamation No. 7918, 50 Fed. Reg. xxx (exact date)

8. Executive Order 13,350. (Assume the material is available in C.F.R.)
Exec. Order No. 13,350, 3 C.F.R. xxx (year), *reprinted in* 3 U.S.C. § xxx (2000). (Note: See Rule 14.7 for examples and forms.)

9. Section 203.211 of title 24 of the Code of Federal Regulations.
    24 C.F.R. § 203.211 (year).

10. Hardy v. Shook, No. 04-123 (Third Circuit, May 28, 2005), Westlaw 13499.
    Hardy v. Shook, No. 04-123, 2005 WL 13499, at *x (3d Cir. May 28, 2005).

11. An article entitled "The Madrid Protocol," written by Neil Jones in
    2004 and located only at www.uspto.gov/web/trademarks/madrid/
    madridindex.htm.
    Neil Jones, *The Madrid Protocol,* (2004), www.uspto.gov/web/
    trademarks/madrid/madridindex.htm.

12. The case *Harper v. Gregory Association,* 535 U.S. 16 (2005), available at
    the website of the U.S. Supreme Court.
    Harper v. Gregory Ass'n, 535 U.S. 16 (2005), *available at* http://www.
    supremecourtus.gov (Note: Per Rule 18.2.2, a parallel citation to an
    Internet source may be given if it will substantially improve access to
    the source cited. The Internet cite may include additional characters.)

13. "Personnel Management: Employee Surveys," volume 70 of the
    Federal Register, pages 54,658-54,660, September 16, 2005 (to be
    codified at 42 C.F.R. part 209).
    Personnel Management: Employee Surveys, 70 Fed. Reg. 54,658-60
    (Sept. 16, 2005) (to be codified at 42 C.F.R. pt. 209).

14. Give the public domain citation (with pinpoints) for the nineteenth 2001
    South Dakota Supreme Court case *People v. Talbot.*
    People v. Talbott, 2001 SD 19, ¶ x, xxx N.W.2d xxx, xxx.

15. Figure 3 of U.S. Patent Number 6102103, filed on February 12, 2005.
    U.S. Patent No. 6,102,103 fig. 3 (filed Feb. 12, 2005).

Exercise for Chapter 7

*Correct the following statements and citations. There may be more than
one thing wrong with each citation, and you may need to create missing
information. Unless otherwise directed, assume that state court cases
are being cited in internal office memoranda.*

1. In Kramer v. Jarvis, 86 F. Supp.2d 342 (Middle District Pennsylvania
    1999), the Court held that ". . . parties to a contract must be competent
    to enter into that contract."

In *Kramer v. Jarvis*, 86 F. Supp. 2d 342, xxx (M.D. Pa. 1999), the court held that "[p]arties to a contract must be competent to enter into that contract."

2. Indicate that the following 2005 Ninth Circuit case was a per curiam decision that was later affirmed by the U.S. Supreme Court the same year: *Bains LLC v. Arco Products Co.*, 405 F.3d 764.
Bains LLC v. Arco Prods. Co., 405 F.3d 764 (9th Cir.) (per curiam), *aff'd*, xxx U.S. xxx (2005).

3. In the following quotation, omit the word "a," pluralize the word "figure," and omit the phrase "for the truth of the statement": "Statements made about a public figure are wrongful if they are made with actual malice, meaning with reckless disregard for the truth of the statement."
"Statements made about [ ] public figure[s] are wrongful if they are made with actual malice, meaning with reckless disregard...."

4. "Battery is a harmful and offensive touching of another." *Nelson v. Campbell*, 347 F.3d 910 (11th Cir. 2003); *Jacobson v. Farley*, 901 P.2d 45 (Calif. 1990); *Vives v. City of New York*, 405 F.3d 115, 122 (2nd Cir. 2004); *Harris v. Consolidated Transportation Department*, 687 So. 2d 118, 121 (Ala. 1994).
"Battery is a harmful and offensive touching of another." *Nelson v. Campbell*, 347 F.3d 910, xxx (11th Cir. 2003); *Vives v. City of New York*, 405 F.3d 115, 122 (2d Cir. 2004); *Harris v. Consol. Transp. Dep't.*, 687 So. 2d 118, 121 (Ala. 1994); *Jacobson v. Farley*, 901 P.2d 45, xx (Cal. 1990).

5. "Defamation is publication of false information about another that harms the other's reputation." *Agostini v. Felton*, 521 U.S. 203 (1997) (dissenting opinion by Justice O'Connor) (original quotation appears in the middle of a sentence.
"[D]efamation is publication of false information about another that harms the other's reputation." *Agostini v. Felton*, 521 U.S. 203, xxx (1997) (O'Connor, J., dissenting).

6. Using appropriate parentheticals, indicate that the following is a 9-0 decision that held that general partners have unlimited personal liability. *Crawford v. Washington*, 367 F.3rd 915, 920-922 (D. C. Circuit 2003), reversed at 541 U.S. 36 (2004).
Crawford v. Washington, 367 F.3d 915, 920-22 (D.C. Cir. 2003) (9-0 decision) (holding that general partners have unlimited personal liability), *rev'd*, 541 U.S. 36 (2004).

7. Show that you emphasized the phrase "whether it arises in tort or contract" in the following quotation: "A limited liability company is an entirely new form of business enterprise that provides full protection from personal liability whether it arises in tort or contract." *Wright v. Benedict Construction Co.*, 701 S.E. 2d 410, 414-416 (Georgia 1988).

    "A limited liability company is an entirely new form of business enterprise that provides full protection from personal liability *whether it arises in tort or contract*." *Wright v. Benedict Constr. Co.*, 701 S.E.2d 410, 414-16 (Ga. 1988) (emphasis added).

8. The Court held that "actual malice must be shown for a public figure to recover punitive damages in a libel action." *Horn v. Banks,* 536 U.S. 266, 271 (2002). Make the following changes: Omit the phrase "for a public figure," emphasize the word "libel," start your quote with the word "malice," and indicate that you omitted a citation from your quote.

    "[M]alice must be shown . . . to recover punitive damages in a *libel* action." *Horn v. Banks*, 536 U.S. 266, 271 (2002) (citation omitted) (emphasis added).

    (Note: Rule 5.2(d) provides the order for parenthetical clauses.)

Exercise for Chapter 8

A. Correct the following. Assume that each number to the left of a question refers to a page within a brief being submitted to a court in your state and that there are no intervening citations between questions. If alternative forms of citation are acceptable, give all. Assume the citations are "standalone" citations.

    1. *Peters v. Colonial General Partnership,* 134 F.3d 909, 913 (Fifth Circuit 1998).

        Peters v. Colonial Gen. P'ship, 134 F.3d 909, 913 (5th Cir. 1998).

    2. Refer to page 915 of the *Peters* case.

        Id. at 915.

    3. Lynne M. Wagner, *Enterprise Law,* Section 101 (second edition 1994).

        Lynne M. Wagner, *Enterprise Law* § 101 (2d ed. 1994).

    4. Refer to section 120 of Ms. Wagner's book.

        Id. § 120.

5. Refer to page 920 of the *Peters* case.
   Peters, 134 F.3d at 920 or
   134 F.3d at 920 or
   In *Peters*, the court also held . . . (assuming *Peters* was discussed in the same general discussion)
6. Refer to section 125 of Ms. Wagner's book.
   Wagner, *supra*, § 125.

B. Correct the following and describe the meaning of any signal used.
   1. But see *Edmonson v. Pearce*, 911 P. 2d 605 (Oklahoma 1993).
      But see Edmonson v. *Pearce*, 911 P.2d 605, xxx (Okla. 1993). *(But see* indicates that *Edmonson* clearly supports a proposition contrary to the main proposition.)
   2. E.g. *Sisler v. TRS Advertising & Marketing Co.*, 809 F. Supp. 2d 18 (District court Connecticut 1999).
      E.g., Sisler v. TRS Adver. & Mktg. Co., 809 F. Supp. 2d 18, xx (D. Conn. 1999).
      (The signal *e.g.* indicates that *Sisler* states the proposition. Other authorities also state the proposition, but citation to them would not be helpful or is not necessary.)
   3. For additional discussion of this topic, see Judith M. Schillings, *Land Use Concepts*, Journal of Land Use and Environmental Law, volume 109, page 166 (2000).
      For additional discussion of this topic, see Judith M. Schillings, *Land Use Concepts*, 109 J. Land Use & Envtl. L. 166, xxx (2000). (Note: In this example, the word "see" is used as an ordinary verb, and thus, it is neither underscored nor italicized.)

C. Correct the following statements made in a brief submitted to a court.
   The Plaintiff in this case has vigorously asserted that her rights under the Fourth Amendment to the U.S. Constitution have been violated. When the police officers employed by the State of California entered her home, they did so without a warrant. Warrantless searches are clear violations not only of the Fourth Amendment but also of California's Tempesta Act. The judicial branch of the federal government has repeatedly upheld the rights of citizens to be protected in their own homes. As Justice Anthony Kennedy of the U.S. Supreme Court has commented, "There is no greater right than that of our citizens to be protected from government intrusion in their homes." Therefore, Plaintiff respectfully urges this Court to grant her motion to dismiss all charges against her.

Exercise for Chapter 9

Use a separate sheet of paper to create a table of authorities for the following authorities that will be cited in a brief. You may need to supply missing information and make corrections in and additions to the citations. You need not provide a reference to pages on which these authorities would appear in the brief.

Cases [Case names may be provided in full rather than in abbreviated form.]

Am. Car & Foundry Co. v. *Kettelhake*, 236 U.S. 311 (1915)
Carden v. Arkoma Ass'n, 494 U.S. 185 (year)
Dura Pharm., Inc. v. Broudo, 539 U.S. 909 (2004)
Hanover Star Constr. Co. v. Metcalf Commc'ns, 114 F. Supp. 2d 90 (S.D. Cal. 1996)
Lumberman's Mut. Cas. Co. v. Elbert, 348 U.S. 48 (1954)
Temple v. Synthes Corp., 130 F.3d 18 (3d Cir. 2001)
United States v. BestFoods, Inc., 524 U.S. 51 (1998)

Statutes

17 U.S.C. § 100 (2000)
17 U.S.C. § 109 (2000)
28 U.S.C. § 1332 (2000)
28 U.S.C. § 1332(a) (2000)
Me. Rev. Stat. Ann. tit. 19, § 909 (year)

Other Authorities

James R. Michaels, *Normative Constructions* 190 (2d ed. 1994)
John B. Oakley, *Prospectus for the American Law Institute's Federal Judicial Code Revision Project*, 31 U.C. Davis L. Rev. 990 (1998)
14 B Charles Alan Wright & Arthur R. Miller, *Federal Practice and Procedure* § 110 (3d ed. 1998)

Chapter Ten: The Final Review

Correct the citations in the following brief and memorandum. The brief is based on an actual brief filed by the U.S. Department of Justice and was revised (and condensed) to provide a "real life" example of a court brief. The author wishes to apologize to the authors of the original brief for these revisions and changes.

You may need to create information such as dates and pinpoints. Follow *Bluebook* rules.

Note the following as you make your corrections:

- Underscoring rather than italicizing is acceptable (as long as it is done consistently throughout a document).
- Pinpoint citations have been added because they are critical and allow the reader to readily locate information.
- Note that periods and commas must appear inside quotation marks.

IN THE UNITED STATES DISTRICT COURT FOR THE DISTRICT OF COLUMBIA

UNITED STATES OF AMERICA,
        Plaintiff,

        v.   Civil Action No. 98-1232 (TPJ)

MICROSOFT CORPORATION,
        Defendant.

_____

STATE OF NEW YORK *ex rel.*
Attorney General ELIOT SPITZER, *et al.*,
        Plaintiffs,

        v.   Civil Action No. 98-1233 (TPJ)

MICROSOFT CORPORATION
        Defendants.

_____

Plaintiffs' Response to Microsoft's Objection to Participation by Professor Lawrence Lessig as an Amicus Curiae

Microsoft has objected to participation by Professor Lawrence Lessig of Harvard Law School as an amicus curiae. Professor Lessig's participation in that role is proper, and Microsoft's objections are ill conceived and unfounded.

I. Background

By Order dated November 19, 1999, the Court invited Professor Lessig to participate as amicus curiae. The Court also permitted the two Plaintiffs and Microsoft each to designate an amicus curiae. In a conference with counsel the day before its Order, the Court explained that it asked Professor Lessig to submit a brief that addresses the legal issue of technological tying. (Tr. 10-11, Nov. 18, 1999 *or* Trial Tr. 10-11, Nov. 18, 1999.) The Court's Order followed the entry of the Court's detailed findings of fact. There is no suggestion in Microsoft's papers, nor could there be, that the amicus process has anything to do with issues of fact.

II. Legal Standard

Although there is no federal rule or statute governing participation by amicus curiae at the district court level, *see United States v. Gotti*, 755 F. Supp. 1157, 1158 (E.D.N.Y. 1991), a federal district court has the inherent authority to invite participation by amicus curiae to assist the court in its proceedings. *United States v. Louisiana*, 751 F. Supp. 608, 620 (E.D. La. 1990); *United States v. Michigan*, 807 F. Supp. 655, 660 (W.D. Mich. 1987). The decision to invite or accept participation by an amicus is committed to the sound discretion of the court. *Allen v. Hall*, 776 F. Supp. 152, 155 (D. S.C. 1974).

The classic role of the amicus curiae is to assist in a case of general public interest, supplement the efforts of counsel, and draw the court's attention to law that may otherwise escape consideration. *Miller-Wohl Co. v. Comm'r of Labor & Indus.*, 694 F.2d 203, 204 (9th Cir. 1982); *see also New England Patriots Football Club, Inc. v. Univ. of Chi.*, 592 F.2d 1196, 1198 n.3 (1st Cir. 1979) (noting that historically, the role of an amicus was "to aid the court in resolving doubtful issues of law"). There is no requirement that an amicus be disinterested. *Funbus Sys., Inc. v. Cal. Pub. Utils. Comm'n*, 801 F.2d 1120, 1125 (9th Cir. 1986); *Hoptowit v. Ray*, 682 F.2d 1237, 1260 (9th Cir. 1982). In this case there is no reason to believe that Professor Lessig is other than disinterested.

III. Argument

A. Microsoft's Arguments

First, Microsoft asserts, without any explanation of its foundation or reasoning, that the Court's Order inviting Professor Lessig's participation is sufficiently broad to constitute a request for proposed conclusions of law. Microsoft also contends that Professor Lessig does not meet requirements to participate as an amicus because he does not have a "particularized 'special interest'" in the legal issues presented in the case but then goes on to argue, seemingly paradoxically, that he should not participate because he is not impartial. (Def.'s Opp'n to Order ¶ 12, Nov. 20, 1999.) These objections are specious.

B. Role of Amicus Curiae

"Amicus curiae" is a Latin phrase for "friend of the court" and an amicus curiae is to be distinguished from an advocate before the court. *Allen*, 776 F. Supp. at 154. Traditionally, an amicus curiae was a neutral provider of information or legal insight to the court, and if partisan, amicus curiae status would be denied. However, the trend, particularly in appellate courts, is to accept and even invite the participation of amici curiae with partisan interests. 4 Am. Jur. 2d *Amicus Curiae* § 6 (1986).

In fact, modern courts have consistently recognized the role of amicus curiae as partisans.

> We recognize that the acceptance of amicus briefs is within the sound discretion of the court, and that by the nature of things an amicus is not normally impartial. Furthermore, if an amicus causes the district court to make an error of law — an amicus who argues facts should rarely be welcomed — the error can be corrected on appeal. Nonetheless, we believe a district court lacking joint consent of the parties should go slow in accepting, and even slower in inviting, an amicus brief unless, as a party, although short of a right to intervene, the amicus has a special interest that justifies his having a say, or unless the court feels that existing counsel may need supplementing assistance.

Strasser v. Doorley, 432 F.2d 567, 569 (1st Cir. 1970).

C. Legal Argument by Amici Will Not Usurp the Judicial Function

That Professor Lessig and the other potential amici may discuss how they believe that the Sherman Act, 15 U.S.C. §§ 1-6212 [or 1 to 6212]

(2000), should be applied to the facts as the Court has found them is neither unusual nor improper, and indeed is the traditional role of an amicus. *See, e.g., Funbus*, 801 F.2d at 1125, in which the court noted that it is perfectly permissible for amicus to "take a legal position and present legal arguments in support of it." Submitting a brief as amici involves *no* delegation of judicial authority or duties and is unobjectionable.

D.   If the Court Believes That Professor Lessig Would Bring a Helpful Perspective to Legal Issues in the Case, It Is Appropriate for Him to Participate as Amicus

"There are no strict prerequisites that must be established prior to qualifying for amicus status; an individual seeking to appear as amicus must merely make a showing that his participation is useful or otherwise desirable by the court. *Louisiana*, 751 F. Supp. at 620. Although some courts have required that the amicus possess some "unique information or perspective," *see Ryan v. Commodity Futures Trading Comm'n*, 125 F.3d 1062, 1063 (7th Cir. 1997), this does not require any particular quantum of expertise beyond the expectation that the amicus will add significantly to, not merely parrot, the contributions from the lawyers for the parties. Moreover, the court in *Gotti*, 755 F. Supp. at 1158-59, rejected a proffered amicus brief that merely parroted the arguments of the defendants in that case.

E.   Microsoft Has Not Demonstrated That Professor Lessig Is Biased Against It

When Microsoft first raised the issue of Professor Lessig's purposed bias, this Court found that Microsoft's bases for its allegations were "both trivial and altogether non-probative." (Mem. & Order 2 [or at 2], Jan. 14, 1998.) In any event, there is no requirement that an amicus be impartial or disinterested. *Hoptowit*, 682 F.2d at 1260; Samuel Krislov, *The Amicus Curiae Brief: From Friendship to Advocacy*, 72 Yale L. J. 694, 699 (1963). Indeed, "by the nature of things an amicus is not normally disinterested." *Strasser*, 432 F.2d at 569. According to at least one expert, "an amicus brief is rarely disinterested; usually it supports one party or the other." Michael Tigar, *Federal Appeals: Jurisdiction and Practice* 133 (2d ed. 1993). Therefore, Professor Lessig's participation as an amicus curiae is proper.

IV. Conclusion

For the foregoing reasons, the Plaintiffs submit that it is entirely proper and appropriate for the Court to invite Professor Lessig to participate as amicus curiae in this case of public importance.

Dated: _____

Respectfully submitted,

_____

MEMORANDUM

To: Francis M. Sullivan
From: Rita Lopez
Re: Liability of Grace Pattersen for Dog Bite
Date: August 18

Factual Background

Our client, Phil Franklin ("Franklin") lives in a residential neighborhood in California. His next-door neighbor is Grace Pattersen ("Pattersen"), who owns a large German shepherd dog, which has previously nipped at a neighborhood child. Two weeks ago, Franklin entered Pattersen's yard and approached Pattersen's door to deliver some mail that inadvertently came to Franklin's house. When Franklin approached the door, he bent down to greet the dog. The dog came out of the unlocked front door and bit Franklin. Franklin received several stitches for the dog bite.

Analysis

Introduction

While many jurisdictions previously followed the view that a dog was allowed "one free bite," this theory has waned as jurisdictions have adopted statutes that impose strict or absolute liability on dog owners for the acts of their dogs. Ward Miller, *Modern Status of Rule of Absolute or Strict Liability for Dogbite*, Annotation, 51 A.L.R.4th 446, 452 (2000). In fact, California has enacted such a statute. Cal. Civ. Code § 3342 (West 1998). That statute provides, in pertinent part, as follows:

The owner of any dog is liable for the damages suffered by any person who is bitten by the dog while . . . lawfully in a private place, including the property of the owner of the dog, regardless of the former viciousness of the dog or the owner's knowledge of such viciousness. A person is lawfully upon the private property of such owner . . . when he is on such property upon the invitation, express or implied, of the owner.

Thus, if Franklin was lawfully on Pattersen's property within the meaning of the statute, Pattersen is strictly liable for the injuries inflicted by her dog whether or not the dog previously displayed any viciousness and whether or not Pattersen knew of such viciousness.

Implied Invitees

One of the key issues in this case is whether Franklin was lawfully on Pattersen's property as an invitee. Franklin was not expressly invited onto Pattersen's property, so the issue is whether he was an implied invitee. The effect of the portion of the statute to exclude its protections to one who is not lawfully on the dog owner's property lawfully is to deny liability to trespassers. *Fullerton v. Conan*, 197 P.2d 59, 63 (Cal. Ct. App. 1948).

The term "invitee" is often construed broadly. For example, an invitation may be implied from customary use or manifested by the conduct of the parties. 61 Am. Jur. 2d, *Premises Liability* § 94 (1986). Similarly, the status of a person as an invitee often depends upon circumstances such as custom or the habitual acquiescence of the property owner. *Id.* Moreover, Restatement (Second) of Torts § 167 (1986) provides that consent to enter another's land can be derived from the relationship of the parties, as is the case with friends, social visitors, or business visitors.

In *Smythe v. Schacht*, 209 P.2d 114, 118 (Cal. 1949), the court found that a child who entered the defendant's property to greet the defendant's son and was thereafter bitten by the defendant's son was on the premises with defendant's implied invitation. The children were playmates and the victim had previously entered the premises on other occasions. Thus, the child was lawfully on the premises.

In the present case, Franklin entered Pattersen's property for the sole purpose of delivering her mail. Social custom and courtesy would dictate that a neighbor deliver misdirected mail. Thus, it seems clear that Franklin was on Pattersen's property with her implied invitation.

Defenses

In adopting its dog-bite statute, California did not intend to eliminate defenses such as assumption of the risk. *Gomes v. Byrne*, 333 P.2d 754 (Cal. 1959). Assumption of the risk requires that a person must know and appreciate the danger involved in an activity and yet voluntarily accept that risk. *Prescott v. Ralph's Grocery Co.,* 265 P.2d 904, 906-07 (Cal. 1954). Similarly, victims are denied recovery in dog-bite cases when they intentionally provoke or tease a dog that then bites them. *Miller, supra,* at 455.

In *Gomes,* 333 P.2d at 755, a salesman approached a yard enclosed by a fence and was followed along the fence by a dog which had barked at him for 50 feet. When the salesman opened the gate and entered the yard, he was bitten by the defendant's dog. The court held that while a person must have actual knowledge of a risk to be denied recovery, such knowledge may be inferred from the circumstances. *Id.* at 756. Because the salesman knew of the dog's hostility and yet voluntarily exposed himself to an obvious hazard, he assumed the risk of being bitten. *Id.* In the present case, Franklin was bitten immediately after Pattersen's door was opened. These facts are clearly distinguishable from those in *Gomes,* in which the salesman had observed a hostile, barking dog and yet chose to enter the owner's land.

Conclusion

Franklin was likely an implied invitee of Pattersen's because he entered her land for the purpose of fulfilling a social courtesy. Moreover, he neither provoked the dog nor did he have actual knowledge of the dog's aggressive nature. In such a case, he will be afforded the protection of California Civil Code section 3342, and Pattersen will have strict liability for the actions of her dog.

Examples of State Cases and Statutes

Notes on cases: Some of the following examples are fictitious, and examples are not given for all cases from each state. Examples marked with footnotes 1 and 3 indicate *The Bluebook* form to be used when citing a state supreme court case or state appellate court case, respectively, when local rules require parallel citations. Examples marked with footnotes 2 and 4 indicate *The Bluebook* form to be used when citing a state supreme court case or state appellate court case, respectively, in any other instance. For states that no longer publish officially, the form shown is that now used in those states. For cases decided before the date on which those states ceased official publication, follow the format of cases shown in footnotes 1 and 3.

 Notes on statutes: Although parentheticals are given following the statutes (showing date and publisher, if publication is not official), most practitioners omit the parenthetical information following statutes. Examples are not given for all statutory compilations for all states. Many examples are fictitious. Note that for many states, *The Bluebook* (Table T.1) indicates a preferred format for statutes, usually citation to the official set.

 In all instances, court rules dictating citation form supersede the following forms.

Alabama*   *Employees' Benefit Ass'n v. Grissett,* 732 So. 2d 968, 972 (Ala. 1998).

      Davis v. State, 720 So. 2d 1006, 1009 (Ala. Crim. App. 1998).

      Alabama statute: Ala. Code § 37-2-83 (1992).

Alaska*   *Bostic v. State,* 968 P.2d 564, 566 (Alaska 1998).
                 Linton v. State, 770 P.2d 123, 126 (Alaska Ct. App. 1994).
                 Alaska statute: Alaska Stat. § 45.55.119 (1990).

Arizona   *In re Am. W. Airlines,* 179 Ariz. 528, 530, 880 P.2d 1075,
                 1777 (1998).[1] or
                     In re Am. W. Airlines, 880 P. 2d 1075, 1077 (Ariz. 1998).[2]
                 Young v. Lee, 214 Ariz. App. 80, 84, 400 P.2d 103, 106
                 (1974).[3] or
                     Young v. Lee, 400 P.2d 103, 106 (Ariz. Ct. App. 1974).[4]
                 State v. Wagner, 194 Ariz. 1, 4, 976 P.2d 250, 255 (Ct.
                 App. 1998).[5]
                 Arizona statute: Ariz. Rev. Stat. Ann. § 28-7906 (1998).

Arkansas   *Powell v. Hays,* 323 Ark. 104, 106, 3 S.W.3d 15, 18 (1995).[1] or
                     Powell v. Hays, 3 S.W.3d 15, 18 (Ark. 1995).[2]
                 Peters v. Boles, 56 Ark. App. 14, 19, 4 S.W.3d 90,
                 93 (1997).[3] or
                     Peters v. Boles, 4 S.W.3d 90, 93 (Ark. Ct. App. 1997).[4]
                 Arkansas statute: Ark. Code Ann. § 5-64-401 (1996).

California   *People v. Ortega,* 19 Cal. 4th 686, 688, 968 P.2d 48, 50, 80
                 Cal. Rptr. 489, 491 (1998).[1] or
                     People v. Ortega, 968 P.2d 48, 50 (Cal. 1998).[2]
                 Chu v. Lee, 33 Cal. App. 4th 80, 81, 229 Cal. Rptr. 6, 7
                 (1995).[3] or
                     Chu v. Lee, 229 Cal. Rptr. 6, 7 (Ct. App. 1995).
                 California statute: Cal. Educ. Code § 8403 (West 1989).
                                       Cal. Prob. Code § 1365
                                       (Deering 1991).

Colorado*   *People v. Altman,* 960 P.2d 1164, 1168 (Colo. 1998).
                 Raney v. Feist, 538 P.2d 89, 97 (Colo. Ct. App. 1990).
                 Colorado statute: Colo. Rev. Stat. § 31-10-408 (1999).
                                      Colo. Rev. Stat. Ann. § 14-10-119
                                      (West 1997).

Connecticut   *State v. Cobb,* 251 Conn. 285, 288, 743 A.2d 1, 4 (1999).[1] or
                     State v. Cobb, 743 A.2d 1, 4 (Conn. 1999).[2]
                 Easton v. Gibb, 245 Conn. App. 14, 19, 618 A.2d 49, 54
                 (1987).[3] or

Easton v. Gibb, 618 A.2d 49, 54 (Conn. App. Ct. 1987).[4]
Connecticut statute: Conn. Gen. Stat. § 29-332 (1999).
Conn. Gen. Stat. Ann.
§ 33-687 (West 1997).

Delaware*   *DiGiacobbe v. Sestak,* 743 A.2d 180, 185 (Del. 1999).
Rose v. Cadillac Fairview Shopping Ctr., 668 A.2d 782,
784 (Del. Ch. 1995).
Delaware statute: Del. Code Ann. tit. 13, § 733 (1989).

District of   *Durham v. United States,* 743 A.2d 196, 199 (D.C. 1999).
Columbia*   District of Columbia statute: D.C. Code § 6-972 (1995).

Florida*   *DiPietro v. Griefer,* 732 So. 2d 323, 326 (Fla. 1999).
Drury v. Jackson, 438 So. 2d 568, 571 (Fla. Dist. Ct. App.
1987).
Florida statute: Fla. Stat. § 421.04 (1993).
Fla. Stat. Ann. § 443.036 (West 1997).

Georgia   *Allen v. Carr,* 216 Ga. 31, 37, 489 S.E.2d 15, 21 (1993).[1] or
Allen v. Carr, 489 S.E.2d 15, 21 (Ga. 1993).[2]
Clay v. Park, 177 Ga. App. 22, 26, 493 S.E.2d 57, 61 (1995).[3] or
Clay v. Park, 493 S.E.2d 57, 61 (Ga. Ct. App. 1995).[4]
Georgia statute: Ga. Code Ann. § 49-4-149 (1998).
Ga. Code Ann. § 38-2-93 (West 1999).

Hawaii   *State v. Maumalanga,* 90 Haw. 58, 60, 976 P.2d 372,
375 (1998).[1] or
State v. Maumalanga, 976 P.2d 372, 375 (Haw. 1998).[2]
Mann v. Kamalu, 89 Haw. App. 45, 47, 590 P.2d 18, 20
(1990).[3] or
Mann v. Kamalu, 590 P.2d 18, 20 (Haw. Ct. App. 1990).[4]
State v. Perez, 90 Haw. 113, 115, 976 P.2d 427, 430 (Ct.
App. 1998).[7,5] or
State v. Perez, 976 P.2d 427, 430 (Haw. Ct. App. 1998).
Hawaii statute: Haw. Rev. Stat. § 516-32 (1997).
Haw. Rev. Stat. Ann. § 516-62 (Lex-
isNexis 1993).[6]

Idaho   *West v. Sonke,* 131 Idaho 133, 136, 968 P.2d 228, 231
(1998).[1] or

West v. Sonke, 968 P.2d 228, 231 (Idaho 1998).[2]
State v. Pilik, 129 Idaho 50, 53, 921 P.2d 750, 754 (Ct. App. 1996).[3,5] or
   State v. Pilik, 921 P.2d 750, 754 (Idaho Ct. App. 1996).[4]
Idaho statute: Idaho Code Ann. § 56-805 (1994).

Illinois
   LeGout v. Decker, 146 Ill. 2d 389, 391, 586 N.E.2d 1257, 1259, 166 Ill. Dec. 928, 931 (1992).[1] or
   LeGout v. Decker, 586 N.E.2d 1257, 1259 (Ill. 1992).[2]
   Martinez v. Mobil Oil Corp., 296 Ill. App. 3d 607, 610, 694 N.E.2d 639, 641, 230 Ill. Dec. 670, 674 (1998).[3] or
   Martinez v. Mobil Oil Corp., 694 N.E.2d 639, 641 (Ill. App. Ct. 1998).[4]
   Illinois statute: 735 Ill. Comp. Stat. 5/1-104 (1993).
                        405 Ill. Comp. Stat. Ann. 5/2-107.1 (West 1997).

Indiana*
   In re Edwards, 694 N.E.2d 701, 704 (Ind. 1998).
   Knaus v. York, 586 N.E.2d 909, 914 (Ind. Ct. App. 1992).
   Indiana statute: Ind. Code § 28-5-1-9 (1998).
                        Ind. Code Ann. § 6-1.1-17-3 (West 1998).
                        Ind. Code Ann. § 28-2-16-17 (LexisNexis 1996).

Iowa*
   In re Wagner, 604 N.W.2d 605, 607 (Iowa 2000).
   State v. Hauan, 361 N.W.2d 336, 336 (Iowa Ct. App. 1984).
   Iowa statute: Iowa Code § 422.86 (1999).
                    Iowa Code Ann. § 524.106 (West 1993).

Kansas
   State v. Valentine, 260 Kan. 431, 433, 921 P.2d 770, 773 (1996).[1] or
   State v. Valentine, 921 P.2d 770, 773 (Kan. 1996).[2]
   Bryson v. Wichita State Univ., 19 Kan. App. 2d 1104, 1107, 880 P.2d 800, 804 (1994).[3] or
   Bryson v. Wichita State Univ., 880 P.2d 800, 804 (Kan. Ct. App. 1994).[4]
   Kansas statute: Kan. Stat. Ann. § 24-621 (1993).
                       Kan. U.C.C. Ann. § 2-316 (West 1996).

Kentucky*

Harrington v. Phifer, 4 S.W.3d 918, 929 (Ky. 1995).
O'Malley v. Gonzales, 6 S.W.3d 404, 418 (Ky. Ct. App. 1998).
Kentucky statute: Ky. Rev. Stat. Ann. § 199.470 (West 1994).
Ky. Rev. Stat. Ann. § 186.412 (LexisNexis 1997).

Louisiana*

Neely v. Turner, 720 So. 2d 673, 675 (La. 1992).
Medicus v. Scott, 744 So. 2d 192, 195 (La. Ct. App. 1993).
Smith v. Jones, 94-2345, p. 7 (La. 7/15/94); 650 So. 2d 500, 504.[8]
Louisiana statute: La. Rev. Stat. Ann. § 23:1142 (1998).
La. Code Crim. Proc. Ann. art. 786 (1998).

Maine*, +

D'Souza v. Garner, 690 A.2d 671, 685 (Me. 1995).
Smith v. Jones, 1997 ME 7, ¶ 14, 685 A.2d 110, 112.[8]
Maine statute: Me. Rev. Stat. Ann. tit. 25, § 2921 (1998).

Maryland

Save Our Streets v. Mitchell, 357 Md. 237, 239, 743 A.2d 748, 750 (1998).[1] or
  Save Our Streets v. Mitchell, 743 A.2d 748, 750 (Md. 1998).[2]
Allied Inv. Corp. v. Jasen, 123 Md. App. 88, 90, 716 A.2d 1085, 1088 (1998).[3] or
  Allied Inv. Corp. v. Jasen, 716 A.2d 1085, 1088 (Md. Ct. Spec. App. 1998).[4]
Maryland statute: Md. Code Ann., Fam. Law § 7-101 (LexisNexis 1999).

Massachusetts

In re London, 427 Mass. 477, 479, 694 N.E.2d 337, 339 (1998).[1] or
  In re London, 694 N.E.2d 337, 339 (Mass. 1998).[2]
Campbell v. City Council of Lynn, 32 Mass. App. Ct. 152, 155, 586 N.E.2d 1009, 1013 (1992).[3] or
  Campbell v. City Council of Lynn, 586 N.E.2d 1009, 1013 (Mass. App. Ct. 1992).[4]
Massachusetts statute: Mass. Gen. Laws ch. 175, § 123 (1988).

Mass. Ann. Laws ch. 183, § 30
(LexisNexis 1996).

Michigan   *Maynard v. Sauseda,* 417 Mich. 1100, 1103, 361 N.W.2d
342, 345 (1983).[1] or
 Maynard v. Sauseda, 361 N.W.2d 342, 345 (Mich.
 1983).[2]
Bass v. Combs, 238 Mich. App. 16, 19, 604 N.W.2d 727,
730 (1999).[3] or
 Bass v. Combs, 604 N.W.2d 727, 730 (Mich. Ct. App.
 1999).[4]
Michigan statute: Mich Comp. Laws § 120.904 (1996).
      Mich. Comp. Laws Ann.
      § 380.1756 (West 1997).

Minnesota*   *Knotz v. Viking Carpet,* 361 N.W.2d 872, 877 (Minn.
1985).
Boldt v. Roth, 604 N.W.2d 117, 120 (Minn. Ct. App. 2000).
Minnesota statute: Minn. Stat. § 50.28 (1998).
      Minn. Stat. Ann. § 541.04
      (West 1988).

Mississippi*   *Lindsay v. State,* 720 So. 2d 182, 185 (Miss. 1996).
Ladner v. Manuel, 744 So. 2d 390, 394 (Miss. Ct. App.
1996).
Smith v. Jones, 95–KA–01234–SCT (¶ 1) (Miss. 1998).[8]
Mississippi statute: Miss. Code Ann. § 65-11-45 (1996).

Missouri*   *Lovell v. B & H Inc.,* 909 S.W.2d 14, 18 (Mo. 1993).
Bryson v. Brant, 925 S.W.2d 689, 694 (Mo. Ct. App. 1995).
Missouri statute: Mo. Rev. Stat. § 367.040 (1994).
Mo. Ann. Stat. § 534.030 (West 1988).

Montana+   *Horn v. Horn,* 165 Mont. 118, 129, 921 P.2d 14, 23 (1996).[1]
or

 Horn v. Horn, 921 P.2d 14, 23 (Mont. 1996).[2]
Dawson v. Walter, 1998 MT 12, ¶ 44, 286 Mont. 175,
¶ 44, 968 P.2d 1312, ¶ 44.[8]
Montana statute: Mont. Code Ann. § 69-1-224 (1995).

Nebraska   *State v. Nebraska,* 258 Neb. 511, 513, 604 N.W.2d 151, 154
(2000).[1] or

State v. Nebraska, 604 N.W.2d 151, 154 (Neb. 2000).[2]
Reinsch v. Reinsch, 8 Neb. App. 852, 854, 602 N.W.2d 261, 264 (1999).[3] or
    Reinsch v. Reinsch, 602 N.W.2d 261, 264 (Neb. Ct. App. 1999).[4]
Nebraska statute: Neb. Rev. Stat. § 72-221 (1996).
                Neb. Rev. Stat. Ann. § 54-101 (LexisNexis 1995).

Nevada[+]   *Shaw v. Gammon,* 113 Nev. 24, 29, 960 P.2d 18, 23 (1998).[1] or
    Shaw v. Gammon, 960 P.2d 18, 23 (Nev. 1998).[2]
Nevada statute: Nev. Rev. Stat. § 243.490 (1999).
              Nev. Rev. Stat. Ann. § 319.350 (LexisNexis 1999).

New Hampshire[+] *Moore v. Tyler,* 89 N.H. 114, 118, 743 A.2d 681, 686 (1999).[1] or
    Moore v. Tyler, 743 A.2d 681, 686 (N.H. 1999).[2]
New Hampshire statute: N.H. Rev. Stat. Ann. § 391:7 (1998).

New Jersey   *Roach v. TRW, Inc.,* 162 N.J. 195, 197, 743 A.2d 847, 850 (1999).[1] or
    Roach v. TRW, Inc., 743 A.2d 847, 850 (N.J. 1999).[2]
Bell v. Bell, 312 N.J. Super. 13, 15, 716 A.2d 318, 321 (1998).[3] or
    Bell v. Bell, 716 A.2d 318, 321 (N.J. Super. Ct. App. Div. 1998).[4]
New Jersey statute: N.J. Stat. Ann. § 17:48-6 (West 1996).

New Mexico   *Barone v. Torres,* 127 N.M. 20, 23, 976 P.2d 21, 24 (1994).[1] or
    Barone v. Torres, 976 P.2d 21, 24 (N.M. 1994).[2]
State v. Ray, 1998-NMSC-001, ¶ 4, 122 N.M. 23, 909 P.2d 112.[8]
Key v. Chrysler Motors Corp., 127 N.M. 98, 99, 976 P.2d 523, 524 (Ct. App. 1994).[3,5] or
    Key v. Chrysler Motors Corp., 976 P.2d 523, 524 (N.M. Ct. App. 1994).[4]
New Mexico statute: N.M. Stat. § 31-2-3 (1997).

New York	*Furch v. Bacci,* 91 N.Y.2d 953, 955, 694 N.E.2d 880, 882, 666 N.Y.S.2d 300, 302 (1998).[1] or
	    Furch v. Bacci, 694 N.E.2d 880, 882 (N.Y. 1998).[2]
	Pryce v. Fowell, 257 A.D.2d 275, 277, 594 N.Y.S.2d 82, 84 (1997).[3] or
	    Pryce v. Fowell, 594 N.Y.S.2d 82, 84 (App. Div. 1997).[4]
	Macy v. Frye, 108 Misc. 2d 994, 997, 438 N.Y.S.2d 156, 160 (Sup. Ct. 1980).[3] or
	    Macy v. Frye, 438 N.Y.S.2d 156, 160 (Sup. Ct. 1980).[4]
	New York statute: N.Y. Dom. Rel. Law § 23 (McKinney 1999).
	                     N.Y. Gen. Bus. Law § 353 (Consol. 1999).

North Carolina	*O'Brien v Matthews,* 280 N.C. 42, 47, 185 S.E.2d 123, 126 (1975).[1] or
	    O'Brien v. Matthews, 185 S.E.2d 123, 126 (N.C. 1975).[2]
	Mill v. Lodge, 5 N.C. App. 657, 659, 169 S.E.2d 36, 39 (1969).[3] or
	    Mill v. Lodge, 169 S.E.2d 36, 39 (N.C. Ct. App. 1969).[4]
	North Carolina statute: N.C. Gen. Stat. § 34-2 (1999).
	                        N.C. Gen. Stat. Ann. § 105-33 (West 1999).

North Dakota*	*Lyon v. Ford Motor Co.,* 604 N.W.2d 453, 455 (N.D. 1996). *Fabricut, Inc. v. Keeney,* 429 N.W.2d 24, 29 (N.D. Ct. App. 1988). *Adams v. North,* 1999 ND 32, ¶ 4, 600 N.W.2d 91, 95.[8] North Dakota statute: N.D. Cent. Code § 28-01-18 (1996).

Ohio	*Columbus Bar Ass'n v. Dye,* 82 Ohio St. 3d 64, 67, 694 N.E.2d 440, 443 (1998).[1] or
	    Columbus Bar Ass'n v. Dye, 694 N.E.2d 440, 443 (Ohio 1998).[2]
	Brown v. Dana, 66 Ohio App. 3d 709, 711, 586 N.E.2d 150, 153 (1990).[3] or
	    Brown v. Dana, 586 N.E.2d 150, 153 (Ohio Ct. App. 1990).[4]
	State v. Harris, 99 Ohio St. 3d 29, 2003-Ohio-1189, 791 N.E.2d 22, at ¶ 14.[8]

Ohio statute:	Ohio Rev. Code Ann. § 4507.3 (LexisNexis 1999). Ohio Rev. Code Ann. § 101.5 (West 1999).

Oklahoma*   *Nation v. State Farm Ins. Co.*, 880 P.2d 877, 890 (Okla. 1994).
Peterson v. Baker, 921 P.2d 955, 963 (Okla. Civ. App. 1996).
Skelly v. State, 880 P.2d 401, 405 (Okla. Crim. App. 1994).
Gray v. Carey, 1999 OK 44, ¶ 4, 978 P.2d 490, 494.[8]

Oklahoma statute:	Okla. Stat. tit. 73, § 83.2 (1991). Okla. Stat. Ann. tit. 68, § 1353 (West 1992).

Oregon   *Tellam v. Birch*, 321 Or. 1, 3, 921 P.2d 380, 384 (1996).[1] or
> *Tellam v. Birch*, 921 P.2d 380, 384 (Or. 1996).[2]

Enders v. Enders, 154 Or. App. 142, 144, 960 P.2d 986, 989 (1997).[3] or
> *Enders v. Enders*, 960 P.2d 986, 989 (Or. Ct. App. 1997).[4]

Oregon statute:	Or. Rev. Stat. § 576.175 (1997). Or. Rev. Stat. Ann. § 657A.290 (West 1994).

Pennsylvania   *Cope v. Miller*, 389 Pa. 116, 119, 716 A.2d 18, 22 (1998).[1] or
> *Cope v. Miller*, 716 A.2d 18, 22 (Pa. 1998).[2]

Hardy v. Sells, 422 Pa. Super. 4, 9, 639 A.2d 909, 914 (1993).[3] or
> *Hardy v. Sells*, 639 A.2d 909, 914 (Pa. Super. Ct. 1993).[4]

Bosworth v. Diaz, 691 A.2d 47, 52 (Pa. Commw. Ct. 1999).
Peters v. Cope, 2000 PA Super. 111.[8]

Pennsylvania statute:	23 Pa. Cons. Stat. § 5303 (1997). 15 Pa. Cons. Stat. Ann. § 224 (West 1996).

Rhode Island*,+   *Estrada v. Walker*, 743 A.2d 1026, 1034 (R.I. 1999).

Rhode Island statute:	R.I. Gen. Laws § 42-64-9 (1998).

South Carolina   *Sullivan v. Pine*, 331 S.C. 190, 199, 502 S.E.2d 19, 29 (1998).[1] or

Sullivan v. Pine, 502 S.E.2d 19, 29 (S.C. 1998).[2]
McKee v. Hall, 331 S.C. 560, 566, 500 S.E.2d 909, 914 (Ct. App. 1993).[3,5] or
  McKee v. Hall, 500 S.E.2d 909, 914 (S.C. Ct. App. 1993).[4]
South Carolina statute: S.C. Code Ann. § 44-7-220 (1985).

South Dakota[*,+] *Meinders v. Weber,* 604 N.W.2d 148, 150 (S.D. 1995).
Hoogestraat v. Barnett, 1998 SD 104, ¶ 5, 595 N.W.2d 900, 904.[8]
South Dakota statute: S.D. Codified Laws § 29A-2-21 (1997).

Tennessee[*] *Booker v. Allen,* 931 S.W.2d 970, 977 (Tenn. 1993).
Davis v. Crane, 918 S.W.2d 887, 892 (Tenn. Ct. App. 1987).
State v. Doyle, 920 S.W.2d 101, 104 (Tenn. Crim. App. 1989).
Tennessee statute: Tenn. Code Ann. § 17-1-304 (1994).

Texas[*] *Kroger Co. v. Robins,* 5 S.W.3d 221, 224 (Tex. 1999).
Peterson v. Reyna, 920 S.W.2d 285, 288 (Tex. Crim. App. 1994).
Allen v. Esterly, 921 S.W.2d 104, 109 (Tex. App. 1995).
Texas statute: Tex. Educ. Code Ann. § 102.12 (Vernon 1991).

Utah[*] *Salt Lake City v. Smoot,* 921 P.2d 1003, 1005 (Utah 1996).
Gregory v. Hendrix, 880 P.2d 18, 24 (Utah Ct. App. 1994).
Allen v. Ray, 1999 UT 240, ¶ 4, 171 Vt. 104, 108, 16 P.3d 1.[8]
Utah statute: Utah Code Ann. § 39-6-37 (1998).

Vermont[+] *Winn v. Riley,* 161 Vt. 16, 24, 743 A.2d 209, 214 (1999).[1] or
  Winn v. Riley, 743 A.2d 209, 214 (Vt. 1994).[2]
Talbot v. Dowd, 2004 VT 111, ¶ 4, 171 Vt. 104, 108, 749 A.2d 406, 409.
Vermont statute: Vt. Stat. Ann. tit. 24, § 1312 (1992).

Virginia *Sheldon v. Drye,* 225 Va. 11, 19, 445 S.E.2d 89, 94 (1995).[1] or
  Sheldon v. Drye, 445 S.E.2d 89, 94 (Va. 1995).[2]
Ruiz v. Harley, 25 Va. App. 16, 20, 486 S.E.2d 90, 95 (1997).[3] or

Ruiz v. Harley, 486 S.E.2d 90, 95 (Va. Ct. App. 1997).[4]

Virginia statute: Va. Code Ann. § 33.1-226 (1996).

Washington   *Brewer v. Brewer,* 137 Wash. 2d 756, 758, 976 P.2d 102, 104 (1999).[1] or

Brewer v. Brewer, 976 P.2d 102, 104 (Wash. 1999).[2]

State v. Hunt, 75 Wash. App. 795, 797, 880 P.2d 96, 99 (1994).[3] or

State v. Hunt, 880 P.2d 96, 99 (Wash. Ct. App. 1994).[4]

Washington statute: Wash. Rev. Code § 80.36.310 (1998).

Wash. Rev. Code Ann. § 35.21.403 (West 1990).

West Virginia[+]   *Farrel v. Bond,* 156 W. Va. 450, 456, 295 S.E.2d 19, 25 (1973).[1] or

Farrel v. Bond, 295 S.E.2d 19, 25 (W. Va. 1973).[2]

West Virginia statute: W. Va. Code § 17A-4-5 (1996).

W. Va. Code Ann. § 19-104 (LexisNexis 19xx).

Wisconsin   *In re Parsons,* 122 Wis. 2d 186, 188, 361 N.W.2d 687, 690 (1985).[1] or

In re Parsons, 361 N.W.2d 687, 690 (Wis. 1985).[2]

Smith v. Jones, 2000 WI 14, ¶ 6, 240 Wis. 2d 220, ¶ 6, 650 N.W.2d 17, ¶ 6.[8]

State v. Schultz, 145 Wis. 2d 661, 663, 429 N.W.2d 79, 81 (Ct. App. 1988).[3,5] or

State v. Schultz, 429 N.W.2d 79, 81 (Wis. Ct. App. 1988).[4]

Doe v. Roe, 2000 WI App 9, ¶ 17.[8] or

Doe v. Roe, 2000 WI App 346, ¶ 27, 239 Wis. 2d 14, ¶ 27, 648 N.W.2d 81, ¶ 27.[8]

Wisconsin statute: Wis. Stat. § 480.08 (1996).

Wis. Stat. Ann. § 70.22 (West 1999).

Wyoming[*,+]   *Ruwart v. Wagner,* 880 P.2d 586, 590 (Wyo. 1994).

Allen v. Eddy, 2003 WY 10, ¶ 6, 81 P.3d 107, ¶ 6 (Wyo. 2003).[8]

Wyoming statute: Wyo. Stat. Ann. § 39-16-210 (1999).

*State no longer publishes officially.

+State has no intermediate appellate courts.

[1]Case from supreme court of the state being cited in a document when court rules require parallel citations.

[2]Case from state supreme court being cited in a document other than when court rules require parallel citations.

[3]Case from state intermediate court being cited in a document when court rules require parallel citations.

[4]Case from state intermediate court being cited in a document other than when court rules require parallel citations.

[5]Appellate court cases are published in same volumes as supreme court cases; thus, parenthetical information is needed to identify the court that decided the case.

[6]LexisNexis has begun publishing a number of state statutes.

[7]Beginning in 1994, Hawaii appellate court cases are also published in West's *Hawaii Reports*.

[8]Vendor neutral or public domain citation form.

Index